HARDWIRED:
TAKING THE ROAD TO DELPHI AND UNCOVERING YOUR TALENTS

Compliments of

Dr. Thomas N. Tavantzis

Innovative Management Development

Thomas.Tavantzis@IMDLeadership.com
610-420-0900
www.IMDLeadership.com

BY
DR. TOM TAVANTZIS

This book is dedicated to my beloved family and friends who have passed on this year.

They include my mother, Helen Tavantzis; my mother-in-law, Alice Taylor; and Lazar Emanuel, president of The Highlands Company.

DISCLAIMER

The instructions and advice in this book are not intended as a substitute for psychological counseling. In the interest of preserving client confidentiality, all clients' names and, in some cases, identifying characteristics have been changed except where permission to use first and last names have been granted. The scenarios, situations, and results are real.

TABLE OF CONTENTS

PREFACE

This book really has two birthplaces, separated by thousands of miles and several decades.

One is in the Philadelphia suburbs. This is where my psychotherapy consulting practice was once located, across the road from the General Electric Space Center.

The other is in Greece. This is where my ancestors are from and where I spent much of my childhood. I return there every year. One of its most famous monuments, Apollo's Oracle at Delphi temple, is said to have borne the inscription "Know Thyself." This maxim has worked its way through Socrates and Plato to the great modern thinkers in the organizational and career development field. Peter Drucker, our modern business Oracle, has restated the heart of the inscription as "Know Your Strengths."

This is not as easy as it sounds. Most people don't know their strengths as well as they think they do.

Over the years, I have found the Highland Ability Battery the best available instrument for assessing one's strengths. It tests your abilities rather than what you believe those abilities might be. Combined with professional interpretation, it can help you find a career path for which you are suited: a road to your own personal Delphi.

Is it easier to develop what we're good at rather than to "remedy" or "cure" our weaknesses?

Drucker and other pioneers of the career and organizational development field, such as Don Super and John Holland and, more recently, Donald Clifford, Marcus Buckingham and Kim Cameron, say it is.

And there is growing evidence that much of what we're good at is hardwired into us at birth and matures at adolescence, and that working against this reality can only produce frustration in our personal and professional lives.

People can't do much about their innate intelligence, or their basic abilities for that matter. True, they can learn new skills or increase their vocabulary. But it is far easier to develop natural strengths and innate social and emotional influences – what we now call "emotional intelligence."

This applies whether you're a middle manager trying to find your best role in a company, or a 30-year-old contemplating a career change, or a high school senior picking a prospective college or major.

The trouble is that very often you don't know what you're good at, or why. Family expectations, roles picked for you by your early employers and casual observations by friends and associates can all get in the way.

We do know what has given us satisfaction in the past. It may be just one aspect of the job we hold now or a hobby. This is the real key to our strengths, like an underground spring we can tap into. Satisfaction comes from using your abilities, and dissatisfaction comes from not being able to use your abilities. Knowing your strengths is the key to planning a satisfying career.

The focus of my work – and of this book – is to make you fully aware of your strengths and how to make the most of them.

1980s BIRTHPLACE

In 1986, my wife and I embarked on a new journey. We decided to uproot our young family (my 6-month-old twin sons and their big sister of 3) to open a practice in a new city for a national psychology group. My practice was based in King of Prussia, Pa., at the edge of a huge shopping mall and within sight of the helipad at the GE Space

Center. My practice involved family therapy. Many of my patients were middle managers about to be laid off at GE.

The themes and emotions they discussed with me were similar: Anger, resentment at having given their lives to the company, fears about seeking a new career. They felt powerless to control their own lives because they had relied on the company to give them a "path" to advancement. They didn't know what they were really good at and were afraid to take the next career step. This, of course, impacted their spouses, their children, their marriages and their health.

As part of the family therapy movement of the 1960s and 1970s, I had come to think of personal problems as the product of our social and organizational systems, not as a condition residing within the individual. A system could be a corporation you had worked for, as well as the family you belonged to.

Few of the GE workers suffered from anything that could have been termed a "pathology." There was nothing "wrong" with them, nothing that could not be helped by getting them back to a place that would allow them to use their strengths and talents productively.

I was becoming increasingly disenchanted at the time with the private practice of psychotherapy, with its emphasis on managed care and medication. The idea of career counseling on a systematic basis, discovering ways that could help large numbers of individuals through their personal crises, seemed appealing.

What did not seem appealing was the field as it then existed.

I had first been exposed to career counseling in graduate school in the mid-1970s. I found it something of a backwater, far less challenging than personal counseling. It seemed a dreary field, and the testing instruments available at the time, including the Myers-Briggs Type Inventory (MBTI), struck me as overly subjective. Many of them were geared to high school and college-age students. They ignored what Drucker called the "New Economy" (to distinguish the shift from the Industrial Age to the Information Age, from factory worker to information worker), and the economy's requirement that people reinvent themselves continually throughout their careers, and not in the way

Madonna has done it. We're talking about hard work that you do yourself, without publicists and image-makers.

With my passionate interest in working with groups and organizations, I started to review the literature to see what had happened in the field of career development between 1978, when I left graduate school, and 1990. Unfortunately, I found that many of the same tools and the same answers were still being used.

I then noticed a small ad for The Highlands Company in the American Psychological Association's monthly magazine. This started a discussion between me and the founders of the company. I had many questions and concerns that needed to be answered before I could take the plunge and fly to Atlanta for a series of training sessions that would last several months! It took six months for me to feel confident enough to register for the training.

The Highlands method emphasizes working with the whole person while treating career guidance as a group enterprise. This all had a special resonance with me because of my upbringing. Although I was born in Astoria, Long Island City, N.Y., much of my childhood and youth was spent shuttling between the U.S. and the cold, snowy, mountainous part of Greece that borders Albania. The concept "Know Thyself" is embedded in Greek philosophy and culture, but the process by which self-knowledge is achieved is very much a community process. The Greek language doesn't even have a word for "privacy" that doesn't have a negative connotation!

In Kastoria. where I grew up, everyone knew everyone else. Roaming the ancient, narrow, cobblestone streets, I could feel the eyes of middle-age and older women sitting in their old Turkish-style (left over from the occupation) homes peeking through the window shades, keeping a close watch on what transpired in the streets. Everyone knew everyone's business, an essential reality in a survival-based milieu.

While I lived there, Greece was a chaotic country on its way to becoming a military dictatorship. The threats of war, political chaos, terrorism and intrigue taught me the vulnerability we all felt. The history of modern Greece is a tale of invasion and war. Kastoria and the rest of northern Greece were not incorporated into the country until the end of World War I. For hundreds of years, they were occupied and governed by the Turks. Inevitably, the Greeks retreated into small, tightly linked groups. Their survival depended on the strength of their families and their communities.

I took my psychological training at the Institute of Anthropos in Athens. My mentors were a world-renowned husband-and-wife team, George and Vasso Vassiliou, respectively a psychiatrist and clinical/social psychologist, who had both trained at the University of Chicago.

The Vassilious were both interested in preventive community psychiatry, focusing on the functioning majority. If you are standing near the river and you keep seeing people drowning, your instinct is to rescue them. Yet what you really need to do is to go upriver and find out why they were getting into the river in the first place!

This approach naturally concentrates on people's strengths rather than their weaknesses, examining how they can function best in the workplace or in society. By the late 1990s, this approach had become widespread and was generally known as "positive psychology" – emphasizing optimism, strengths and values.

In the business world, strength-based thinking has become so accepted that it forms the basis of a new field known as "Positive Organizational Behavior."

Not surprisingly, I have found that managers who know their own strengths are far better at recognizing the strengths of those working for them.

When I lead a seminar, I always ask the participants what they do automatically when they first encounter a problem. If it's a corporate seminar, I also ask how they contribute best to a work team in the first five minutes of a crisis.

In most cases, the people are baffled. They have a sense of how they process information and how they operate, but they have never really articulated it.

THEN AND NOW

"This is like deja vu all over again."

— Yogi Berra

Today, as in so many other periods in our history, the economy remains sluggish for many, many people. Unemployment, downsizing, pay cuts, corporate greed, government ineptitude, unpaid furloughs – these are all with us. Gallows humor prevails as people see their "401ks becoming 201ks." Recently, a young coaching client of mine in her first job after college came in shocked and almost in tears as she described the abruptness of layoffs at the company she worked for. "People who had been there for 15 years were being escorted out of the building."

I had the feeling I was repeating my earlier experience with layoffs at GE, only this was worse. If we are to learn from history, we know that people internalize employer downsizing and layoffs. They become negative and blame themselves. The question becomes how to navigate the turmoil and not get caught up in the downward spiral. Instead, use the moment – as hard as it may be – to look inside yourself and develop a conscious awareness of your talents and embrace your abilities. You can stay on top of your career plan and navigate even today's rough economic waters.

My focus – and the focus of this book – is to bring you into conscious awareness of your strengths and how you can best use them, and to assist you in recognizing the variations in abilities that exist among all of us. Our gifts are there to be developed and make our contribution unique and productive. Most people look at their abilities and end the search by focusing only on their personality traits: Extrovert, Introvert, Conscientious, Open, Closed, etc. Yet, we know instinctively that there is more to us than our personalities.

In the following chapters, I will share with you a few examples of people who had their initial work with me in processing their Ability Battery results. The examples reflect the issues and challenges at different stages in people's careers and how the Ability Battery helped them. I hope you will see yourself in some of these people, and get support to begin your understanding of your abilities; to be productive and contribute from your talents and help others to work from their strengths.

PART 1

INTRODUCTION

"But the bravest are surely those who have the clearest vision of what is before them, glory and danger alike, and yet notwithstanding, go out and meet it."

– Thucydides

"We hire people for their skills, but the whole person shows up for work."

– Chester I. Barnard

This book is about people who start to think about their careers in a new way by understanding their strengths in a new way. The people range from an IT project manager to a graphic designer, to a sales director and to a high school senior.

All began by taking the Highlands Ability Battery. I explained the results to them, and together we interpreted them in light of the work they were doing then or the work they might do in the future.

For them, it was the start of developing a Personal Vision, a process that usually takes several months.

Part of this development required them to reflect on their values and interests and part of it consisted of looking back at their Family of Origin and at career decisions they made at key Turning Points in their lives.

Our families are incredibly powerful influences on our lives. We often take the same paths as our parents and grandparents, or even our older siblings. However, even if their decisions were right for them, they may be wrong for us.

Most of our work together was simply absorbing and processing the results of the Battery, learning to use them as a new lens with which to view the way they operate. Simple to say, but not easy to do.

For example, if you are high in Classification – we'll get back to this in a few pages – you can become impatient with associates who are slower to analyze information, or with me for keeping you waiting a few pages. However, these same associates will be more likely to draw on past experience as a guide in ways that you cannot. Knowing your own strengths and sensing the strengths of your co-workers or direct reports is a win-win for you and your employer.

For example, a top executive of a major pharmaceutical company shared his results with his direct reports to help them get a greater sense of his operating style. Accepting that he couldn't be all things to all people, he then asked how each in turn could consciously contribute to supplement and complement him for the greater good of the team.

Some of these chapters are about people who were in the right job but just wanted to find ways to do it better. Others were considering a different job in their company or perhaps in a completely different field.

They all were starting on an exciting journey of discovery.

* * *

A Personal Vision

Before moving on to a more detailed discussion of Abilities, I should caution you that discovering and analyzing them is only the first step toward developing a larger Personal Vision. Some of the people in the book continued their work with me over several months as a way to reach this eventual goal.

A Personal Vision is a detailed statement of how you want to live your life. It tells you who you are; what you like to do; what you think is worth doing; and what you want to accomplish. It needs to be written down and reviewed often.

The Personal Vision is made up of eight key factors:

- Driving Abilities
- Personal Style
- Skills
- Interests
- Values
- Goals
- Family of Origin
- Stage of Development

All are needed to help you shape your life and your career. The first three are determined with the help of objective testing, and all must be integrated with each other to understand how complex we are as human beings. Eliminate any of them and you can't build the structure.

How do you get to a Personal Vision and what does one look like?

You start by assessing your **Personal Style** and **Abilities** and by using your creative unconscious to design an environment in which creativity can be fostered. There is nothing mysterious about this. The greatest discoveries on the planet are all products of both the creative mind and the logical mind.

To build a vision, you need to step back and get a fresh perspective on work and life. Don't say, "Oh, I'll get around to that," because you won't. You have to set aside time and energy to focus on creating an articulated description of yourself.

Lisa, a 60-year-old trainer for a major health insurer, did this for my Advanced Career Development graduate course at Saint Joseph's University in Philadelphia. She said, "I see myself more clearly than I have ever seen myself in my life. And I find that exhilarating and so exciting."

Creating your Personal Vision requires some time away from noise – both in your head and outside. But it is not a solitary process. Even if you do much of this work one-on-one with a coach/counselor, you will find yourself drawing on those around you: family, friends, mentors, people in fields you are considering.

I am always gratified at the group energy I see when some of the work in my course is done in a seminar setting or in a workshop of corporate executives.

Our lives are lived with others. Whether we come from a small mountain town or a sprawling suburb, we come to know who we are by interacting with our families, friends, peers, classmates and co-workers. Those around us see us through their own eyes – with their own perceptions, needs, hopes and dreams. This makes getting a perspective on what we are really good at a difficult task.

"Why can't we hear ourselves?" asked Lisa. "I don't know," I responded, "but we can't. What I do know is we can't do it alone. We need other people to guide us."

ASSESSING
YOUR STRENGTHS

*"Ah, why did I not pay attention when they were building
the walls? But I never heard any noise or sound of builders.
Imperceptibly they shut me from the outside world."*

— Constantine P. Cavafy
Walls, translated by Rae Dalven

The Highlands Ability Battery traces its history to studies done in the 1920s by Johnson O'Connor, an engineer at General Electric who had a Harvard degree and two pet theories. One theory was that workers would be more efficient if assigned to tasks that were best suited to their abilities. The other was that natural abilities are hardwired and can be measured objectively.

O'Connor set out to design objective performance tests to measure abilities used on the plant floor, such as a dexterity test for meter assemblers. Eventually, he founded his own testing organization.

The Highlands Company has succeeded in transferring the work samples developed by O'Conner to the Web. The Highlands Ability Battery (THAB) measures hardwired abilities through a series of timed work samples. It is administered online and takes about three hours to complete, although it does not have to be completed at one sitting.

In my work with my clients, the Battery is the first part of a three-part process. It is followed by a 34-page report, and then by a two-hour feedback session in which I help the client understand the significance of each element of the results.

ASSESSING YOUR STRENGTHS – THE FIRST STEPS

Some of the abilities we test are called the **Driving Abilities**. These are part of our hardwiring. These abilities are so powerful that we must take them into account when considering what role we should play at work. Think of them as the four-lane highways of the mind.

They determine how you absorb information and solve problems. Do you operate more through logic or through intuition? Do you tend to think in abstract terms? Do you come up with many ideas to solve a problem, or do you think of one or two and stick with them? How good are you at visualizing and manipulating objects in three dimensions?

The Driving Abilities influence:

- The school or work environment that feels most comfortable to you
- How you learn new information most easily
- How you solve problems and make decisions most efficiently
- How you communicate with others most effectively

You will want to consider the Driving Abilities in identifying or changing careers, choosing new directions in your current career, or reentering the workforce. Highlands has named each of the Driving Abilities. They are: **Classification, Concept Organization, Idea Productivity, Spatial Relations Theory** and **Spatial Relations Visualization.**

Classification – sometimes called "inductive reasoning" – is designed to measure the method by which your right brain absorbs a plethora of related and unrelated facts and observations and comes up with a solution. People who score high in Classification tend to arrive at solutions to problems more quickly than those with low Classification. But their solutions may not be any better, and their operating style often reflects impatience with those who work more deliberately.

People with high Classification are often successful in jobs that place a premium on thinking on your feet: Trial attorneys and emergency room physicians are good examples. People with low Classification are more likely to look to their past experiences for solutions to problems. And they have an easier time drawing on them.

Concept Organization uses the left hemisphere of the brain and is sometimes called "deductive reasoning." Rather than look for information everywhere at once, people with high Concept Organization deal with information one step at a time. People with high Concept Organization tend to be able to express themselves easily and to predict the future by describing a series of predictable consequences. Project managers, engineers and computer programmers, for example, are likely to have high Concept Organization. Like people of high Classification, they are less able to access their past experiences.

Idea Productivity measures the flow and number of ideas a person is likely to have when seeking a solution to a problem. It doesn't measure the quality of the ideas, but the results can be very helpful in determining a sound career choice. A person with high Idea Productivity may be well suited to a job in sales or marketing, but he is less likely to adjust to a career requiring intense concentration, such as accounting or surgery.

Top executives tend to be low in Classification, Concept Organization and Idea Productivity. The most successful have a collegial style that draws out the best ideas in their direct-report associates and helps them set priorities when they put the ideas into practice.

Spatial Relations is the ability to perceive three-dimensional objects floating, twisting and turning in space. People with high Spatial Relations ability are called structural thinkers. Many are scientists, engineers and, of course, architects. Physicians also tend to score high in this area: They can conceptualize the human body and its parts, and how they work.

People scoring low in Spatial Relations are usually abstract thinkers, more comfortable with concepts and ideas than with objects and structures. They are often lawyers or teachers. Top executives tend to be abstract thinkers with low Spatial Relations ability. Someone scoring high in Idea Productivity can make an excellent salesperson, but she would almost surely be less successful – or at least find it more challenging – managing a sales operation. And the number of ideas a person generates does not bespeak their quality. If you're a corporate executive, your success as a manager probably lies less in your being able to do everything well and more in your ability to choose co-workers and direct reports who are strong in areas where you are weak. You may want your accountant to be someone with low Idea Productivity. And you certainly don't want your surgeon to come up with new ideas in the middle of an operation!

Your **Personal Style** determines the roles you are best suited to play in the workplace. Are you an **Introvert** or an **Extrovert** or – like some of us – something in between? Are you a **Generalist** or a **Specialist**, i.e., a hedgehog or a fox? Do you prefer to work with a variety of people or tasks, or would you rather work alone or concentrate on one area? The world and the workplace need a variety of styles.

What is your **Time Frame Orientation**? Are you more comfortable with longer-term projects or with those that yield immediate, tangible results? In fact, the test most commonly used to measure Time Frame was originated in World War II by British psychologists who wanted to see who would make the best spies behind the

German lines. They realized that the best spies would be able to wait for months and years for the right time to act.

In today's world, we associate low Time Frame with firefighters, and engineers— people who are gratified by work environments that pull for short-term, problem-solving results driven behavior and high Time Frame with five-star generals and CEOs of global companies, who need to plan and work with projects that are seven to 10 years away.

Take the case of George, a training and development manager at a global coffee distributor. George found that his short Time Frame orientation, which had frustrated him when mapping out his career, was not a character defect but simply a part of him that separated him from others. When he discovering this in one of my seminars, he said, "It made me change my habits and my behavior." Soon, he had mapped out a caffeinated career plan that had him moving closer to the company's corporate headquarters in California and working his way up in the company, one step at a time.

The Battery also told George that he was a Generalist working in a Specialist's position – a hedgehog (Generalist) in fox's (Specialist) clothing. He was frustrated teaching the same thing all the time. The solution: keep adjusting his teaching methods, even those that worked, and look for a position in the company that would give him more varied experiences, "something that lets me interact with different groups, to be part of a group that looks at what systems we need."

THE OTHER FACTORS

S kills are sometimes confused with abilities, and the line between them can be blurry at times. For the most part, skills can be learned and abilities can't. Building skills through training and experience makes up for gaps in our abilities. Skills can be compensation for low abilities or extensions of high abilities.

Skills are often taken for granted. My job is to encourage you to remember and own those that you already have. Analyzing your career as a set of skills enables you to assess other jobs or careers in terms of the skills you already have. The concept of "transferable skills" is crucial to flexibility.

Skills also blend with our Interests and leisure pursuits. Interests are those things you are passionate about, regardless of where and how you express them. An activity that you have always treated as a hobby may, in fact, incorporate some skills that can be used in your current career or in a different and more satisfying one.

Even when we recognize our real strengths, we can be blocked from using them by expectations and ideals imposed from outside. These pressures can come from our Family of Origin or from the demands of an employer. Either source can force us into roles that suit needs other than our own. Each pressure can develop into a "system."

The effects of the Family of Origin on our choice of careers are often subtle. Rarely does a parent "pressure" a child to go into a particular career. Instead, a parent responds to the child's personality and intelligence and makes more subtle signs and suggestions. The child's responses to these signs are largely unconscious. They are that portion of the iceberg that lies below the emotional water line.

If, for example, your father had formed a business that failed, you might unconsciously seek the security of a 9-to-5 job even if it is not the best place for your talents and skills. The ability with detail work that made your mother a wonderful seamstress could well be embedded in your DNA, ready to emerge and help you in working as an architect. A good exercise is to reflect on what your family taught you about handling stress and about decision-making.

Assessing the effects of your family need not involve deep mining of painful experiences. It should be more a question of conducting low-key, productive family interviews centered on the work experiences of your parents, siblings and other relatives.

In researching your Family of Origin, you will also want to be particularly sensitive to "turning points" in your parents' lives and in your own. These are the Career Stages when individuals tend to feel the stress that brings on major life changes. People tend to make the same decisions at the same stages as their parents did – often with unfortunate results.   (In the next chapter, I explain Career Stages more fully.)

While pressure to pursue a particular career can come from outside, it can also come from inside ourselves in the form of our Goals and Values. For example, if you have risen to school administrator, a return to teaching can mean a reduction in pay or in prestige. And it can certainly divert and distort your lifelong aim to serve as school superintendent and as a candidate for higher administrative office.

Developing a Personal Vision means examining your Goals and Values in more detail than you ever have before. Without your Personal Vision, sorting out your own goals from those set for you by your family, your employer or society is impossible. Only by freeing yourself from the expectations of others can you develop a Personal

Vision. Your vision should not be based on what other people – family, friends or employer – may think. This does not mean, of course, that you should ignore their counsel and their "reading" of your abilities. It means balancing your own needs, and your own conception of yourself, with theirs.

Take the case of Charles, a top-performing salesman for a medical supplies company. Charles is one of about 300 working adults who have taken my graduate Career Development class. Many of them hold key positions in their companies but find that the class is their first opportunity to reflect deeply on where their lives and careers should go over the next several years.

In working on his Family of Origin, Charles was reminded that his father had always been involved in music. When Charles was younger, he had played several musical instruments and had been in a band. Under the pressures of school, work and then family, he had drifted away from music. But his scores measuring his Musical Abilities were so high that he said to himself, "I just knew I needed to use that outlet." As he formed his Personal Vision, he made sure that music would again be a part if it. A career in music alone would not make sense, but he was encouraged to pick up the guitar again.

As Charles' experience shows, your Personal Vision requires that you integrate what you already know about yourself with what you discover in completing the Battery. The process can direct and galvanize practically every aspect of your life.

UNDERSTANDING
CAREER STAGES

"Bean by bean the sack is filled."
– Greek proverb

One of the Eight Factors central to developing a Personal Vision is understanding where you are in your Career Development cycle. However, to analyze your Ability Battery results, as we do in the coming chapters, we need to know how you got to where you are and where you want to go.

Although circumstances play a significant role, particularly in today's unpredictable economy, most of us tend to go through the same series of Turning Points in our lives. These are times when we are particularly open to new ideas or to change, either career-related or personal. We ask ourselves, "Who am I?" "What is my role?" or "How can I best contribute?"

In this book, we observe a variety of individuals at different points in their career development. But Turning Points can apply to personal development as well. Turning Points can lead to starting a new business, to marriage or divorce, or to venturing into an entirely new line of work. They can occur at various stages, from our high school years into and past retirement. The stages generally occur every seven to 10 years, and each stage usually lasts one to three years.

The stress and unease that are common at Turning Points can incite creative movement toward your true self. If you try to deny or bury your impulses, they can cause stagnation, or even misguided change that is wasteful or destructive. Developing or redefining your Personal Vision is the key to making these periods productive. Changing to a more fulfilling career is a far wiser response in these periods than simply getting a new car or even moving to a different city.

Uncertainty in the economy can also play a role, sending us "stay the course" messages that frustrate what may be a natural Turning Point. Our friends can also send us the same "don't make a change now" messages. But the pressures at our Turning Points are pretty much hardwired into us, even in times of stress. They are not erased by circumstances around us.

My experience with several thousand corporate participants has convinced me that they are always relieved to find that there is a predictable sequence in the midst of what appears to be chaos. In a sense, their anxiety is about the unknown in their futures. By staying in the present and accessing and inventorying their strengths and resources, they can approach the future differently.

You may recall from your college psych or health course that the renowned psychologist Abraham Maslow spoke of a hierarchy of human needs, ranging from the most basic – personal safety, shelter, food – to the most advanced, e.g., self-actualization. Yet even in the throes of meeting our basic needs, we strive to increase the complexity of our social relations. Freud once spoke of Love and Work as the only things that really matter, and our Turning Points are where these most come into play. Having a cognitive map – even an imperfect one – can help us in navigating new territory. It's our personal GPS for the roads ahead.

Turning Points are usually grouped as follows:

High School to College (ages 17-18) – This is where the first career decisions are usually made. It is also where we are most vulnerable to pressures from our Family of Origin. It is the time when real knowledge of our skills and abilities is most helpful. In some cases, our abilities may be similar to those of a family member, but they may lead us down a different path.

College to the World of Work (ages 22-28) – If the first career decisions weren't made at the first Turning Point, they need to be made here, or else we will remain attached to the family and become "stuck."

Age 30 Assessment (ages 28-33) – This is the first real evaluation of where our career path is taking us. It may also be the point at which we are starting a family. This is the point at which people mention to me the real desire to focus their talents and find out what they really want to do.

Midlife Transition (ages 38-45) – This can be a period of great growth or of total disaster. Our children may be approaching their own first Turning Point and getting ready to leave home. We may see the limits in our world of work and start to look at other ways to express our values or seek fulfillment. It can also be a time of divorce, depression or drugs. The blurring of traditional male/female roles at home and in the workplace makes this middle Turning Point a greater challenge than before. It can make balance more difficult to achieve in your life – there is a greater tendency to "want it all." This can also be a time when you begin to realize that you can no longer ignore your values and goals, or your strengths and your passions. Perhaps you pick up the guitar again, express yourself creatively, volunteer to help others in need in a meaningful way. This becomes a time to say "hello" again to your core self.

Age 50 Assessment (ages 50-55) – The Midlife Transition is significant for all of us and, perhaps, may be more significant for women because it is the point at which they pass childbearing age. Their parents may have died. If their assessments were put off at the earlier stage, the issues that were ignored then may force themselves to the surface here. Also this is the point at which people start to experience feelings of mortality and wonder more about what is ahead, perhaps feeling as though they have another meaningful career in them. They can awake from what seems to have been a light sleep, feeling perhaps that for the past 15 years they have been sleepwalking but now feel enlivened by what is ahead and want to make the most of it.

Age 60 Assessment (ages 60-65) – Traditionally, and most recently in the industrial era, retirement has been a pinnacle to reach. However, we know now that the key is to see it as something more than the absence of work. It can be a period of great fulfillment. The foundations laid in the previous assessments come to fruition. We may reach the height of our powers, as our passions, values, abilities and personal style flow together in an integrated fashion. Or we may feel great emptiness. If you have lived this long, statistics indicate you have a good chance of making it into your 80s. The quality of your Personal Vision will do much to determine how those years are spent.

Age 70 Assessment (ages 70-75) – This can be a time for "giving back," for passing our knowledge, experiences and values to the younger generations. And we can still assess and correct decisions we made earlier. Our productivity remains high, and we want to, and can, contribute. As my mentor humbly said to me when she was in her early 70s, "for some reason, the younger folks believe I can still contribute."

The Final Transition (ages 80-?) – This is a time of almost inevitable change from independence to partial or total dependence, but it is also a time of assessment and introspection. Have we fulfilled our Personal Vision? Have we been faithful to our values? Have we left a message of hope and fulfillment? Here, we can see the patterns in our life and work and continue to contribute to our families and friends. Once again, the Personal Vision we have developed can help us maintain our connections and our productivity.

Where are you at this point in your own career? Are you in a period of transition? At a recognizable Turning Point? In Part III of this book, you will find simple but worthwhile exercises that will help you identify and consider the themes, phases, satisfactions and influences on your career.

WHAT'S AHEAD – THE CASE STUDIES

The following 16 chapters are drawn from consultations I conducted over an 18-month period with people who sought me out privately, or who participated in group programs conducted as part of organizational efforts by several companies.

Each chapter is a distillation of a one-time, two-hour consultation with each individual over his or her assessment results. The chapters are organized in the order in which the clients were positioned in their development cycles.

Some of the 16 went beyond the original consultation and entered one of our structured career vision programs; others chose to work through the program on their own. All had a profound moment, an experience during the discussion of their abilities that made a difference in their lives. Almost all felt that "aha" moment that suddenly pulls disconnected fragments into a crisp picture: a picture that allowed them to move on and achieve another view of themselves.

Although many of these clients experienced profound change as they went through the process, our focus here is not on the outcomes but more on the concerns, challenges and hopes they reflected at the start of their journey. The 16 are spread over the adult career life cycle and represent issues we all face at our Turning Points. These people will speak to you through their stories and help you arrive at some answers for yourself.

The answers are in the variations in our abilities and the fascinating ways in which we strive to be productive, to contribute and to be competent. As I find myself saying often to workshop participants, "No one wakes up in the morning and says to himself, 'How can I be incompetent today?'" We all strive to be judged competent. Ultimately, this book tells us how we learn our strengths and how rediscovering what is often hiding in plain sight can be the basis for changing our lives.

✳ ✳ ✳

PART 2

Jill's Results

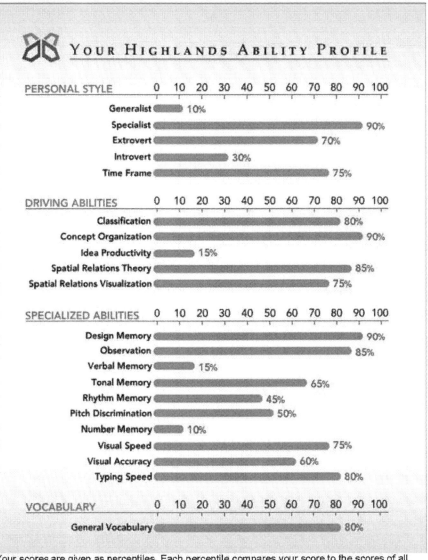

YOUR HIGHLANDS ABILITY PROFILE

PERSONAL STYLE   0 10 20 30 40 50 60 70 80 90 100

- Generalist — 10%
- Specialist — 90%
- Extrovert — 70%
- Introvert — 30%
- Time Frame — 75%

DRIVING ABILITIES   0 10 20 30 40 50 60 70 80 90 100

- Classification — 80%
- Concept Organization — 90%
- Idea Productivity — 15%
- Spatial Relations Theory — 85%
- Spatial Relations Visualization — 75%

SPECIALIZED ABILITIES   0 10 20 30 40 50 60 70 80 90 100

- Design Memory — 90%
- Observation — 85%
- Verbal Memory — 15%
- Tonal Memory — 65%
- Rhythm Memory — 45%
- Pitch Discrimination — 50%
- Number Memory — 10%
- Visual Speed — 75%
- Visual Accuracy — 60%
- Typing Speed — 80%

VOCABULARY   0 10 20 30 40 50 60 70 80 90 100

- General Vocabulary — 80%

Your scores are given as percentiles. Each percentile compares your score to the scores of all persons who have taken the same worksample.

THE CASE STUDIES

"How come you are going barefoot on the thorns?"
— Greek proverb

I. Jill, 18, Entering College
Looking to College and Beyond

The middle years of high school are an ideal time to take the Ability Battery. Even in the finest school systems, guidance counselors are too thinly spread to provide the individualized career advice we all would like for ourselves. They also lack access to sophisticated tools like the Ability Battery.

The sooner you know your abilities and strengths the better off you are, and the sophomore high school year, when the average child is 15, is the earliest stage at which the Battery is effective. I had my three children take it when each was a second-semester junior.

"What's the point if the student isn't into it at the time?" you may ask. The point is that as time passes, the student will return to her results many times. Each time, she will pay more attention to the findings. Equally important, the student should share the report with her parents and listen to the digital recording of her feedback. Everyone will then have a keener understanding of the student's

strengths. These may be very different from the results they antici-
pated, and very different also from the parents' own strengths.

For the student, there can be an added benefit. People may
stop asking, "What will you major in?" or "What are you going to
become?" and on and on.

I began by having Jill go through her assessment with a
Dynamometer, an instrument that has been around in psychology for
a long time and is currently used in sports rehabilitation and physical therapy. The subject squeezes the device with either hand several
times with whatever strength she can muster. She is asked to increase
the pressure each time.

The dynamometer doesn't measure hand strength so much as
persistence. Recent studies from the world of experimental psychology using dynamometers, or Grip tests, correlate scores with general
physical health, stamina and tenacity. For us, these tests help us to
assess how persistent we can be in completing tasks that turn out
to be more frustrating or complex than we originally thought they
would be.

Jill's Grip score was fairly high, and I told her, "When goals are
clear, Grip scores tend to go up. When goals are unclear, scores are
more likely to be low. Compared with other women your age- other
18-year-olds-your score in persistence is relatively high."

"I'm not sure what I want to do yet or how I'm going to do it," she
said. "I want to do something with international relations, diplomacy
and helping others. Either by helping them through government service or doing some nonprofit work, like the Peace Corp or... I'm not
really sure there. I have volunteered a lot with the Red Cross, learning
about farming by working on them and recently became proficient
at canning. I just liked learning about other countries, how people
think and live in other countries."

I asked her what classes she found most interesting in high school.

"I took mostly political science classes as my electives and really
liked those. I enjoyed my science classes."

"And you've also done a lot of travel, right?"

"Yeah, I did travel with a friend for a summer in Australia working odd jobs. Worked our way through Cambodia working and learning about farming. I lived in Italy for a month. In Rome, I learned a lot of Italian. It was easy especially since my Mom's family is Italian." She also said she had chosen her college partly because it had an international studies major.

"So if you were to think about some sort of fantasy dream job, what would that be? Would it be traveling? Would it be working with other cultures?"

"I want to travel because it's fun," she said. "Maybe teaching other people about different ways to cultivate crops…be part of helping to build-up underdeveloped nations. Helping people be self-sufficient. Something like that."

"Sounds good."

Jill had thought of herself as an Introvert and was surprised to see herself score as an **Extrovert** on the Ability Battery. I explained to her that this was perhaps the one score that can change based on an individual's desire to operate in the world in a certain way. "One theory is that people learn skills to be more comfortable in the extroverted world. It's a possibility."

I also said it could fluctuate "depending on the circumstances, depending on how you're thinking and feeling at the time. The family can also play into it. As you get out of the family, you can become more who you were meant to be.

"On the Extrovert side of the world, it's about being plugged into the interpersonal world, getting energy from people and exchanging ideas and talking things out as they appear in your head. The Introvert side of the world is about thinking things through, plugging into yourself to get energy and you may or may not share them or disclose them to other people."

"Well, I think I definitely can get energy from other people more than I can from myself," she said, "but I tend to think things over more in my head rather than talking them out."

The test indicated that Jill was definitely a **Specialist.**

Some 70 percent of us are primarily Generalists. Generalists share a common response to most situations. If I say the word "dime," to a Generalist, nine times out of 10 the response will be "nickel." If I say the word "dime" to a Specialist, the response may be "Susan B. Anthony" or "buffalo head" or something else indicating a personal preference.

"Specialists are always going to see things differently and uniquely," I said. "It's a little tough to live with that sometimes."

"Yeah, I guess that is why I first think things in my head. I have a hard time explaining myself sometimes to other people because I think about things in a different way. I want to understand things really well."

We then returned to the Introvert/Extrovert question. I asked her what role she liked more in her Red Cross teaching role. Did she prefer to perform or remain behind the scenes? She said she found it "a lot more energizing" to be on the teaching and performing side.

"A Specialist/Extrovert feels a kind of a push and pull in two different directions," I told her. "She spends time by herself investigating, researching and understanding something, but then she wants to talk about it with someone and display her new knowledge or skill."

In **Time Frame**, Jill came out in the upper end. This indicated she was able to think ahead five to seven years fairly easily. In her case, that meant a choice between graduate school and, perhaps, the Peace Corps.

I told her, "You can certainly handle an assignment working over a period of years for the Peace Corps or some sort of implementation of a plan for agricultural changes in a country and its people.

Jill said she had hated the time pressure of the **Classification** section of the Battery, but she had still gotten a high score. Clearly, she was a quick problem-solver. I said, "Think about a trial attorney, think about an emergency room physician, or think about an Emergency Manager who has to make quick decisions on the disaster scene. OK, this tent here, station that group of workers over there."

I think it is important to try to take the dream of a young person and to link it in concrete terms to his or her results on the Battery.

She had what I called a "Rubik's Cube of a brain," and – as I always do with clients with high Classification – I warned of the dangers of arrogance toward those who lack this trait: "You're in class, and the teacher hasn't finished describing what the problem is, and you're wondering why everyone isn't catching up to you? Does that sound familiar?"

"Yeah, yeah. That makes sense."

"There should be nothing on this that's a surprise," I told her. "What it's supposed to do is validate some things that you have experienced or felt or thought about." This is a key point: 99 percent of the folks who come in are not dazzled by new discoveries but rather the clarity, the illumination of parts of themselves and their strengths in ways they had not connected or fully considered.

Jill's **Concept Organization** score was even higher – 90th percentile. In the teaching field, this high capacity for deductive reasoning could make coming up with logical processes to teach others. "This is a little more methodical and step-by-step, but when you're doing presentations, when you're organizing your thoughts inside your head and then writing them out, it comes out pretty smoothly. So in your head, you're very organized; outside, your room and your desk might be a complete mess, but inside your head you know where everything goes."

As I often do, I noted again how people with high Classification and Concept Organization might be prone to procrastination for different reasons – either they find holes in every plan they come up with or they have to analyze over and over to make sure they have covered everything.

In **Idea Productivity**, Jill was low-range, low enough that "you do want to be in a role where it's about focus and follow-through much of the time."

The other two Driving Abilities are **Spatial Relations Theory** and **Spatial Relations Visualization.**

Spatial Relations Theory shows one's ability to see theoretical relationships that exist in the working of the mechanical universe: Basically, how systems work.

This applies to both mechanical systems and interpersonal systems. Successful diplomats and mediators, for example, might be expected to score high in this ability. In general, so do people more comfortable dealing with abstract ideas.

A high score in this area can also indicate the ability to design tangible structures but not necessarily to build them.

Spatial Relations Visualization more directly measures one's ability to work in the world of physical objects. In contrast to Spatial Relations Theory, a high score in this area sometimes correlates with an impatience with roles and tasks that deal mainly with ideas or relationships.

Medical students (93 percent) and physicians generally score high in both abilities. They can conceptualize the human body and how it works and – in most specialties – they want to have a tangible, hands-on relationship with it.

Jill was in the 70th percentile for Spatial Relations Theory, which meant she could easily grasp the theory involved in farming production. She was in the 80th percentile for Spatial Relations Visualization, which would have been an advantage in a career such as engineering. Definitely a career that allowed her to be working with tangible objects and seeing practical results, like canning, building ovens, etc.

In the **Specialized Abilities**, she ranked low in **Design Memory and** high in **Observation**.

"People who score like you do," I told her, "are people who can pick up on nonverbal cues, can scan the environment for cues and easily see what is missing or out of place…"

The **Specialized Abilities** play a major role in our personal and work lives.

Design Memory measures your ability to recall a pattern or picture represented in two dimensions. People low in this area may find it more helpful to get information through the written or spoken word.

Observation measures your ability to pay close attention to visual details, which can include body language. A high score here is often associated with artistic ability.

Verbal Memory measures your ability to learn new words or to recall what you've read. Those who score low in it often compensate by reading out loud, listening to books on tape or associating words with pictures.

Tonal Memory measures your ability to remember what you hear, including tunes and tonal sequences. Scoring high in it means you can easily learn to play a musical instrument or master the accent of a foreign language.

Rhythm Memory measures your ability to recall rhythm patterns. It also relates to kinesthetic learning, or learning through movement. Your score here, for example, might well correlate with mastering a golf swing.

Pitch Discrimination measures your ability to note small differences in pitch and is often related to perceptual discrimination in all the senses. It is useful in such varied activities as gourmet cooking or working with small machines. **Tonal Memory, Rhythm Memory** and **Pitch Discrimination** are sometimes referred to as the **Musical Abilities**. If you score high in all three, you will almost surely be frustrated unless you can find some outlet for them.

Number Memory measures your ability to recall facts and data and to use numerical information to solve problems and make decisions.

Visual Speed and Accuracy measure your ability to read and interpret written symbols. Those who score high in it are usually comfortable handling large volumes of paperwork or dealing with columns of figures.

Jill's Verbal Memory score was in the 15th percentile, indicating she had some challenge recalling what she read but would not learn as quickly in this area as she would in some other areas. I told her that taking notes in the margins of her books would be helpful.

Her Tonal Memory was high, however, indicating that she was more able to learn by remembering what she heard, such as a lecture. "You might want to practice the skill of reflecting back what words you think a person said just so they know they were heard," I told her.

Jill's Rhythm Memory score was mid-range, which I told her would be helpful in learning through hands-on experience. Her Pitch Discrimination score was also mid-range. "Pitch Discrimination is also about the creative side of you because pitch is creativity, there's that kind of formula.

"So what you have in this formula," I told her, "is you have the Specialist piece, you have the Idea Productivity low-range, and then you have Design Memory low, Observation is high, and Pitch Discrimination is mid-range. The creative side of you has to come out and that's different from the standard engineer. It could be the person who designs a new kind of outdoor oven."

She also had a high **Vocabulary** score. "That's a big finding and it certainly should influence you to think about going pretty far in terms of your career."

JILL'S DISCOVERIES

"OK, what are the big things? The big findings are that you're in the Specialist world. We have an interesting hypothesis that you're in the Extrovert world in what's called a performing personal style, which is someone who has an area of expertise who enjoys getting up and telling people about it and communicating about it.

"You have a longer Time Frame so you can think ahead strategically, at the same time being results-oriented. Four of your five Learning Channels are high. You have many ways of taking in new information and have as well a thirst for learning new things. It is a significant push from within as well as being a very quick learner!

"Your Spatial Relations Visualization ability is a pull toward being involved with some tangible outcomes, but that could be for a company that makes things, or building up the technological side of the world"

We then discussed how Jill should use the Ability Battery in the days and weeks to come.

"It takes three or four months to figure out how this works and really what you're supposed to do initially is look back at the report and start seeing it in terms of the choices that you make. Like when you're problem-solving, how quickly you jump to the conclusion or how you need to structure it and then as you start to see yourself, you're going to be drawn to roles that you can contribute best from.

"It means being in a role where you can be a problem-solver, where you can perform, where you can become an expert, where you have some creative outlets for yourself."

Most of my work with high school juniors and seniors involves meeting with them one-on-one to discuss the results. I then suggest that they share with their parents the digital recording that they receive along with the report. In Jill's favor was the fact that her father had taken the Battery several years earlier and used his results as a guide in his career. So Jill's parents were comfortable with reviewing the recording and the report and providing guidance in that way.

Jill might be going against the grain of introversion in the family. She is looking for a position in work settings where she can be in the role of performer, engaging with people and making things while using her creative abilities.

She can succeed in roles in which she can learn new things quickly and with little stress. She also has strong pulls toward roles in which she is engaged in rapid-fire problem-solving and decision-making. Her strong Vocabulary suggests she should aim high in her career goals.

Takeaways

- For coaches: Almost everyone who gets feedback on the Battery is dazzled not so much by new discoveries as by the clarity, the illumination of parts of themselves and their strengths in ways they had not connected or fully considered.
- For you: Introverts can learn skills to operate better in the Extrovert world.

- For you: People with high Classification and Concept Organization might be prone to procrastination for different reasons. They find holes in every plan they come up with or they have to analyze over and over to make sure they have covered everything.

Detour: GRIP

Grip is a measure of physical energy, not strength. It reflects your ability to mobilize your strength and drive to accomplish what you set out to do. In this sense, it is a measure of your determination and stamina. Unlike the other ability work samples, Grip is somewhat affected by your mood and mental state at the time your Grip is measured.

Let's say you score in the medium to high range on Grip, as Jill did. This indicates good stamina, drive and persistence in accomplishing what you set out to do. In many people this indicates that they need less rest from fatiguing activities than people lower in Grip. This score means that you will keep going in activities, even when they are more difficult than you thought when you started.

With a high score in Grip, it is sometimes possible for people to persist and keep driving in activities, even when it is in their interests to give up.

A score closer to the mid-range is frequently more adaptive. It means that even when you are heavily engaged in something, you are more able to step back and evaluate whether you are making progress.

Medium-high Grip is a very positive indicator of motivation and drive. When you are clear about your goals, and when you can take stock from time to time about whether you are making progress toward them, you can use this ability to its best advantage.

* * *

DON'S RESULTS

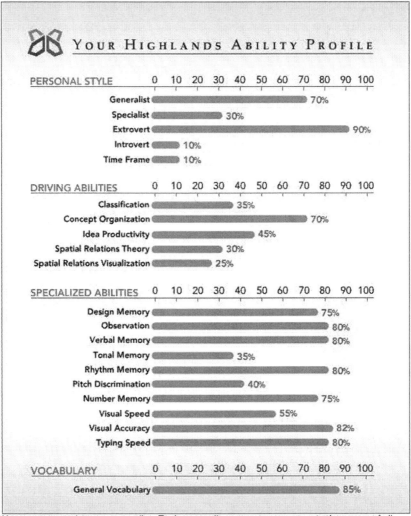

YOUR HIGHLANDS ABILITY PROFILE

PERSONAL STYLE — 0 10 20 30 40 50 60 70 80 90 100

- Generalist — 70%
- Specialist — 30%
- Extrovert — 90%
- Introvert — 10%
- Time Frame — 10%

DRIVING ABILITIES — 0 10 20 30 40 50 60 70 80 90 100

- Classification — 35%
- Concept Organization — 70%
- Idea Productivity — 45%
- Spatial Relations Theory — 30%
- Spatial Relations Visualization — 25%

SPECIALIZED ABILITIES — 0 10 20 30 40 50 60 70 80 90 100

- Design Memory — 75%
- Observation — 80%
- Verbal Memory — 80%
- Tonal Memory — 35%
- Rhythm Memory — 80%
- Pitch Discrimination — 40%
- Number Memory — 75%
- Visual Speed — 55%
- Visual Accuracy — 82%
- Typing Speed — 80%

VOCABULARY — 0 10 20 30 40 50 60 70 80 90 100

- General Vocabulary — 85%

Your scores are given as percentiles. Each percentile compares your score to the scores of all persons who have taken the same worksample.

"When the student is ready, the teacher will appear."

— Buddhist proverb

II. Don, 23, a Recent College Graduate
Finding Ways to Look at Your Options

Here is an interesting situation of a young person who had taken the Battery when he was going off to college. Upon graduating and returning to the area, he decided to pursue his feedback consultation. It may not matter when one gets this information. What had happened, I believe, was a curiosity about the results that needed time to ripen.

This story is interesting from another perspective. Don graduated from one of the top three large public high schools in Pennsylvania, but he had received little career guidance aside from a group-administered Interest Inventory in his junior year. Guidance counselors' time was consumed by problem students and the college admissions process.

Don first took the Battery when he was a freshman in college. He did so as a result of his parents' encouragement. For whatever reason – distance, timing – he did not receive a feedback consultation. In our meeting, it was clear, however, that he had kept several of the key findings in mind. He had attended a small private university in the South, majoring in psychology and Spanish. He had traveled and studied abroad extensively and then graduated into the current tough economy with some ideas of what he wanted to do, but not a definite direction.

Graduate school seemed next on the horizon, but he also wanted to explore academic positions in international studies, and organizational psychology and also sports marketing. The time now seemed ripe to him to better understand the results and use the data to plan his career.

Don, the youngest of three children, always excelled in sports and academics without effort. School came pretty easily to him. Don had very few work experiences before and during school.

OUR CONVERSATION

As Don and I were chatting early in the session, he told me he was in a college basketball fantasy league "and that's been my main hobby recently."

I quickly pointed out that our hobbies are often a clear indication of the strengths we can use in the world of work.

"The draw there is kind of using statistics, analyzing and probabilities and things," I said. "You want to pay attention to those kinds of events, those kinds of situations because they can tell you a lot about what your interests are, what excites you, what brings you some pleasure and enjoyment. You can begin to see a pattern and incorporate that pattern into what's out there."

"Right," he said. "I've always been good with numbers."

I suggested that he "write down anything that draws your interest, the title of a book, the geographic environment you want to work in, what kind of personal environment you would feel much more comfortable in and be drawn to.

"Do you like a multi-generational environment or do you prefer different socioeconomic environments?

"Now on an interpersonal basis, you want to look at what kind of relationships and what kinds of situations with people drain you, and what kinds of relationships and what kind of interactions energize you.

"Let's talk about family and values," I said. "Every family has a culture, and every family has what I call hidden loyalties. 'Do I pursue something that my Mom was doing? Do I pursue something that my Dad was doing? Do I pursue something that my grandparents were doing?' Because there are themes that run through families.

"So in your family, you grow up with a certain set of core values and then, as you branch out, you go to school and then you're out on your own. Values change. So it's truly critical that what you do for a living is consistent with your own personal values. You take a kind of an inventory of 'What are my personal values? What are the things I want to get up in the morning to do?'

"That way, what you do for a living becomes part of your own personal value system rather than it just being a job.

"Goals are also a factor. I don't mean getting up in the morning and paying the bills. I mean what you want to do for a living, how you want to live your life."

In terms of the Career Development cycle, he was clearly at the second Turning Point. "All right, I've got this degree, now what do I do with it?" Not knowing a direction right now is not unusual. It's fairly normal and typical. You need a process to help you think through it.

"It isn't just your abilities, it isn't just your interests, it isn't just your knowledge. It's a combination."

Don scored as a Generalist, in the 70th percentile. "This suggests that as a Generalist you enjoy working as part of a team, working on a project, working as part of an organization or a department. At work settings where there are a number of tasks and roles that you move between during the workday.

"You would find a great deal of enjoyment and satisfaction by working on that team where at one time during the day you are contributing statistics, and later in the day where you're the guy asked to analyze the personnel on a team, or on a project."

Don scored very high as an Extrovert, 90th percentile. That surprised him. But as so often happens in these sessions, the clues had been there all along.

"Yeah," he said. "Usually when I'm taking a test, I'm, like, 'Oh, this is boring.' I kind of want to be with other people. So I'm being more extroverted."

"It's going to be really important," I told him, "that you be able to break up those long periods of more solitary work with interactions. Calling somebody and going to lunch, whatever it is. You do need that interaction. Your preferred mode of interaction is talking and listening. Very different from you, someone who is more introverted prefers to read and write; they get their information that way."

Here we find an interesting pattern we call Group Influencing and Persuading, when we have high Generalist coupled with high extroversion. This is a person who contributes by being drawn to an interpersonal environment where there is lots of interaction, discussion and many different roles available.

Don had a relatively short Time Frame, 10th percentile, "meaning that you tend to like to see the immediate results of what you do. By immediate, it could range from the next five minutes to maybe three to six months. But for you to stay focused and not get distracted, you really need to be on projects that have a fairly quick turnaround."

"Sometimes I procrastinate," he said. "Could that be the result of (short) Time Frame?"

"Yes," I said, "waiting until the last minute is sometimes a factor. Things don't seem real until you've got the adrenaline going."

Don scored in the lower range in Classification, 35th percentile, which I said enabled him to "persevere, to take your time to understand something, take time to be patient with other people and be patient with yourself. To be able to receive information and be able to listen to what other people have to say rather than disregarding what they say and going off on your own."

His score on Concept Organization was much higher, 70th percentile, indicating that this would be his main asset in problem-solving. "This is a very logical, sequential way of thinking," I said. "Very linear, predictive. People who are planners, whether you're working as an event planner, project manager or you're an urban planner or in environmental work, you can see the consequences of the next step."

Don realized this was why he was so interested in developing a rating system for college basketball teams.

I added that Don's high Concept Organization could also play into his tendency to procrastinate, because people with that ability sometimes delay making decisions because they think they may not have enough information.

Don was in the mid-range in Idea Productivity, 45th percentile, indicating that he had a strong flow of ideas but could not be thinking out of the box all the time.

"Now just to give you an example of some areas where the kind of score you have, they include management, facilitating, administrative work, accounting, engineering, law and some areas of banking. You don't have to be in a situation where you're reinventing the wheel all the time." The strength of the mid-range ability score indicates a person can draw from both extremes, i.e., generate ideas but stay focused.

Don scored in the 30th percentile in both Spatial Relations Theory and Spatial Relations Visualization, meaning that he was drawn more to the world of relationships than of mechanical things. "This is much more in tune with occupations involving information-sharing, data-gathering, knowledge," I told him. "You don't have to have a tangible product, 'something I made.'"

I asked him whether when he was younger and his bicycle broke down, "did you want to get in there and figure out how it worked or how to fix it?"

"Not really," he said.

Among the Specialized Abilities, Don had a very high score – 75th percentile – in Design Memory and even higher, 80th percentile, in Observation. Design Memory would enable him to easily absorb information from, say, a statistical chart. The Observation score would be a real asset in helping him work with people, since he could easily absorb what they were wearing, facial expressions, body language, etc.

He also was in the high range on Verbal Memory, 80th percentile. "Learning, taking in information by reading, interpreting written symbols is a strength of yours," I said. "It also makes learning specialized languages fairly easy for you, too. This is also interesting when you consider how strong the extroverted world is for you. My guess is that your lower Idea Productivity helps you stay focused on something you are reading. And, of course, it helps that you learn so easily through this Learning Channel – and as we will see your strong abilities in visual dexterity and processing help you move quickly and accurately across the words."

Don's Tonal Memory score was in the 35th percentile, which he didn't see as terribly important because he had never been interested in playing a musical instrument. However this lower percentile also indicates that stressless learning through auditory channels was not a strength. His Rhythm Memory was considerably higher, 75th percentile, indicating that he could learn through body movements.

He recalled wrestling in high school. "I would be on the bottom, but I knew what to do and where to go to get out without ever opening my eyes," he said.

"Exactly right. That would be your Design Memory and your Rhythm Memory knowing where your body's going to go and where it needs to go."

In Pitch Discrimination, he was in the lower mid-range, 40th percentile. "This is a measure of the other senses," I told him, "visual acuity, taste, smell and touch." This meant that his senses weren't that distracting to him, but I cautioned that if he were part of a creative design consulting team, he might want to include some people with higher Pitch Discrimination.

In Number Memory, he was in the 75th percentile, hardly remarkable for someone so comfortable with statistics, but a great validation for a 23-year-old of his comfort with numbers.

In Visual Speed and Visual Accuracy, he was in the higher ranges— 55th percentile and 80th percentile, respectively – indicating an ability to quickly process and handle administration and paperwork. His Vocabulary score, 85th percentile, was in the range of people successful in fields including higher education, law and public relations. Here, his Extrovert style as well as his high Concept Organization also could be an asset as he can organize his thoughts and communicate the subtleties of his position to others in a positive, helpful manner. Interestingly, Don also thought of teaching as a profession. And among his college peers, he was voted to be the one most likely to become a college professor!

"Don, you have all the Learning Channels working well for you, so you are a fast learner. On interviews, you want to emphasize how quickly you can get up and over the learning curve."

We moved on to discuss some occupational roles that tended to correspond with particular ability sets or personality types. We went over them in the order that each seemed to match his profile, from the strongest to the weakest match.

The first set of abilities that could be grouped to consider – his Generalist/Extrovert personal work style coupled with his low Classification and high Concept Organization as well as his being in the abstract world (low Spatial Relations Theory and Spatial Relations Visualization) – was the one that emphasizes working with and through others potentially as an upper-level manager/leader. Here, his Generalist score as well as his Extrovert tendencies would help him to "understand people and organizations at an intuitive level.

"You can instinctively know how to motivate and encourage people, deal with people problems and get a team to operate efficiently with each other. The manager is able to let others who may have strong abilities shine in their respective roles while you pay attention to the all-important operation of the team." Obviously when we describe this role to a young, inexperienced person, we aren't saying that he can be a high-level manger in a company tomorrow but rather that with experience (low Classification) he will be able to easily move into such a role in the future. Having experience in an area would enhance his confidence in leading a team.

A second set of abilities could contribute to occupational roles that called for planning for projects and teams. "Your high Vocabulary score allows you to communicate easily and well up and down the organizational ladder as well as your ability to put ideas into a logical sequence (high Concept Organization) could be an asset here as well as your low Time Frame – a pull to get things finished."

Additionally, his Generalist, Extrovert and mid-range Idea Productivity would also assist him in marketing/sales roles. His score in Idea Productivity also seemed more suited to nonfiction than fiction, e.g., writing an article for a professional psychology journal or planning International Study Abroad groups for a university, or planning a marketing campaign for a sports team.

"As a Generalist," I told him, "you can also focus on the needs of the company or team or project, often setting aside or delaying a personal agenda to do so. Concept Organization helps you organize work tasks and details in an orderly way. Being low in Idea Productivity can help you stay focused. Verbal Memory assists you in retaining information acquired through written communications such as e-mail.

"Another area to view as a way to contribute would be from a financial perspective, building on and developing your abilities where your strong Visual Speed and Visual Accuracy and Number Memory could be an asset. This could mean going on to graduate school and getting your M.B.A., or developing your statistics background and working on a team of researchers."

DON'S DISCOVERIES

Don was surprised by his high Concept Organization, but once he thought about his past behavior, it made sense. However, he had not considered all his strengths or integrated his strengths: being a Generalist, Extrovert, high Concept Organization, high Visual Abilities, high Verbal Memory, high Design Memory. Also, his ability to focus (lower Idea Productivity and lower Classification) coupled with his high Vocabulary! He also had not considered how his low Classification and being in the abstract world impacted him.

Don said he hadn't particularly thought about managing others but had thought about planning, citing an annual Super Bowl party he had been putting on for years. He also recalled the joy he felt when he organized groups for special events at college. He also recalled being able to do statistical analyses for a term project and then writing up and presenting research reports easily in college.

"That's what writing and presenting is about," I told him. "Whether it be facts in a research paper or investigative reporting and writing. And the investigative part could be for a particular campaign, or a particular marketing project or research in terms of developing some new processes or gathering new data."

Summing up, I said, "This gives you some blueprints, but you will need to do research and fill in the details. Conduct informational interviews with people in careers you may be considering. If you think in terms of a jigsaw puzzle, I'm giving you a kind of border and you have to fill in the details."

Takeaways

- Our hobbies are often a clear indication of the strengths we can use in the world of work.
- Every Family of Origin has a culture, and every family has what I call hidden loyalties.
- Those who score high on Concept Organization need to find ways to use this in their study.

ALICE'S RESULTS

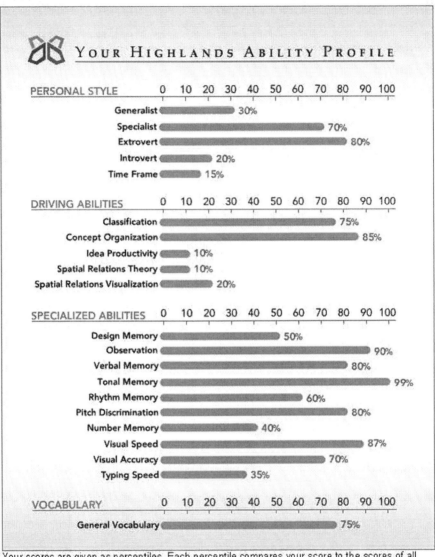

Your scores are given as percentiles. Each percentile compares your score to the scores of all persons who have taken the same worksample.

"The camel does not see its own humps"
— Greek proverb

III. Alice, 29, a Project Coordinator, Software
At a Crossroads: Moving into the 30s Turning Point

Here was a very gifted person trying to figure out her direction with no outside help. How many other young people have the same dilemma, without direction, without a road map, relying on their own rich but undeveloped resources to navigate through the complexity of our society? Essentially, she was a strong Specialist trying to fit into a Generalist niche that doesn't meet her needs, an underused, multi-talented problem-solver looking for a role to contribute.

Alice was 29 and a project coordinator — basically a general trainer — at a software company.

OUR CONVERSATION

"I research training in support of a department's need," she said, "either in direct response or in response to a corporate goal. I go out to dinner with vendors, select the best solution and go through to implementation of data collection. There's also a lot of logistics. I do corporate events and event planning."

"OK," I said. "Give me some idea of roles that give you energy and roles that you can do but may take more effort."

"I like to see the big picture with fresh eyes and come up with a solution from scratch," she said. "At some point I do enjoy going to a level of detail. I'm very organized, but doing the same thing over and over again makes me want to poke my eyes out."

Alice helped pay her way through school by working at Neiman Marcus and other high-end retail stores. She attended community college, getting a degree in marketing. She worked in corporate communications at a utility company and "loved that job."

I asked her why.

"I realized I loved to travel; it really excited me. I was young. I'd get sent to some strange city on my own and I had to figure it out. It was very empowering."

After two years at the utility company, she joined the software firm in the corporate communications department and transferred to human resources in less than a year. She was doing a rotation through human resources and finishing her master's degree in HR but was thinking of transferring to the M.B.A. program.

I asked her where she wanted to be in five years.

"I'm really stuck right now," she said. "I feel like I'm at an education crossroads and a career crossroads. Do I finish my HR master's? Is this the right company for me? I feel like I could be in HR the rest of my life, but my real passion is marketing."

"The Specialist needs time in their own head," I said, "and when you combine it with the Extrovert, it's like, 'OK, I'm going to practice, I'm going to paint, but then I want to put on a show of what I painted for the public.' If I'm extroverted and I'm writing a book, it would be great to take breaks and have some people to exchange ideas with.

"It's a push and pull in two different directions. Usually, when you have a Specialist, you have an Introvert. Extroverted Specialists are really great at rallying people around a vision and getting them excited about it and selling them on the idea."

Alice scored low in **Time Frame,** and I told her, "On a personal note, that makes it a little challenging to think about education. If you break it down into shorter segments, it seems more manageable. Low Time Frame is about immediacy, being in an environment where you can drive for results and turn things around and move on to the next thing."

She scored high in **Classification,** and we discussed how this quick problem-solving ability can play out in the corporate world.

"High Classification people are the ones who sit at meetings and when you're doing your presentation, they've already figured out where you're going. They're fidgeting; they take out their BlackBerrys. There can be a high level of arrogance."

I worked hard to listen to Alice on multiple levels. When I give feedback to clients, I am responding not only to *what* they have told me during their history but also to *how* they told their story as well as my experience. (See my profile in the Appendix and note that I am an experiential problem-solver and decision-maker with high Idea Productivity.)

I always tell the person who shows high in Classification that a downside can be appearing arrogant. The question is always "Will a person own it?"

"Well, I catch myself and I try to fix it," she said. "I judge people really quickly and I'm usually proven right, which is why I did OK in recruiting. I'm trying to back off a little on that because I have such a black-and-white view, like, 'You're an idiot; you're not; you're nice.' So, yes, I'm working on that. I don't always say out loud what's in my head." With an internal sigh of relief, I felt that we could now work more closely.

"It's tempting, though," I said. "If you were completely introverted, it would just stay there. Low Classification is more about living in the present, needing more information to solve problems."

Alice was also high in **Concept Organization**, which meant that she could quickly solve a problem through inductive reasoning, then use her more deliberate deductive reasoning power to explain how she had done so. She had a consultative problem-solving style, able to size up a situation quickly and make recommendations.

"Often this style is a pretty good match for a role in marketing in a fast-paced environment that thrives on short time frames and results," I told her. "A draw for a role that "It's pretty demanding to have this particular problem-solving ability," I said. "Do you get to use it in your daily job?"

"Yes. My boss definitely knows I have it because she'll say that 'whenever I have some weird thing, I'll throw it at Alice.' I don't know that it's enough of my job, though."

"Well, the goal of the Ability Battery is to think in terms of a five to 10 percent increase in the use of your abilities per day," I said.

She scored low in **Idea Productivity** and looked at this almost as a conscious decision. "I think I come up with one or two of my perfect solutions and then I stop. It's like, 'These are perfect, you guys can keep talking, but I have the answer in my head right now and I can just save us all a lot of time.'"

What she was doing, it seemed, was using her high Classification to solve a problem and then coming to a logical solution rather than brainstorming alternatives. As we often see on teams with folks in the room with high Idea Productivity come into conflict with the person both high in fast-paced and logical problem-solving while low in idea production.

This conflict can be constructive if team members are acting with awareness of their own and others' abilities and the impact these abilities have on others.

Alice scored low in both **Spatial Relations** areas, clearly putting her in the abstract world, "the world of face-to-face interaction, the world of CEOs, managers, trainers, HR people."

I asked her what she did for hobbies, and she mentioned singing in choirs and painting murals.

"And how critical are you of your murals?" I asked.

"Oh. My God. I'm like a crazy person. I always find fault."

I had spent about an hour going through Alice's report before the feedback session. Usually, I make some notes and develop some hypotheses about the person, with whom I may only have had a brief telephone conversation earlier or no contact at all.

In planning the consultation, I had seen additional abilities that complemented her expressed perfectionist strengths/tendencies.

"Being high in Classification has its drawbacks," I said.

"Yes. When I'm cooking, I always think I could have done it better."

She scored in the 50th percentile in **Design Memory** but higher in **Observation**. This was particularly helpful in her art, making her more sensitive to minor changes in the visual field. **Verbal Memory,** the most traditional Learning Channel, was high, 80th percentile.

She was even stronger in **Tonal Memory.** "If you hear something, it stays," I told her. "You go to class, you don't take any notes, you listen to the lecture and it's in your head. Most people, if you look around in a staff meeting, after five minutes, their eyes glaze over. That channel isn't working very well. It gets saturated pretty easily.

"This goes with Classification. In your head, you're solving a problem while people are talking." I went on to ask her to consider how she can be more present when working with people. Alice hears and remembers what people say but may not give the impression of being present! This is both the gift and the dilemma of the person with high Classification and high Tonal Memory.

Alice's Musical Abilities were also so high I told her she'd need an outlet for them: She scored in the 99th percentile in **Tonal Memory** and 60th percentile in **Rhythm Memory** and also high in **Pitch Discrimination.** As an artist, she probably wouldn't produce a lot because of her low Idea Productivity, "but you're going to be very focused in terms of what comes out.

ALICE'S DISCOVERIES

All told, Alice had a short learning curve in terms of new things, which would be helpful since she was nearing the key career decision stage that often occurs around 30.

"It's a good thing you're in graduate school," I told her, "because that's where you specialize. Undergraduate liberal arts school is always hardest for the Specialist.

"Let's try to pull some of this together. We have a strong Specialist/ Extrovert type, someone who needs to gather a depth of experience in an area before feeling confidence. But at the same time, she wants to demonstrate her expertise with others working in a short-term, results-driven environment, a fast-paced environment where she wants new problems coming at her. She can quickly diagnose what the problem is and describe the steps others need to take to address it.

"Bringing this set of abilities to another level happens when we tie in her out-of-the-box solution thinking and her creative prowess to her high Vocabulary and the ability it gives her to communicate with a wide range of folks up and down the corporate ladder.

"Sounds like quite a package. No wonder you are having a hard time putting this together. You have so much going on!"

For people with multiple abilities, I often suggest that they continue in a structured career vision program. Fortunately, Alice would be continuing with us within her company.

When feedback sessions work right, the clients leave the room beaming, as Alice did, energized by their abilities and the interplay that they see for perhaps the first time!

Takeaways

- **For you:** The goal of the Ability Battery is to think of a five to 10 percent increase in the use of your abilities per day. This means seeking out roles that allow you to play to your strengths and recognizing those areas where you will need to compensate.
- **For a team setting:** Conflict can be constructive if team members are acting with awareness of their own and others' abilities and the impact these abilities have on others.
- **For coaches:** When pointing out what you see as a client's strengths, pay close attention to whether he really owns it or just says he does. This is where the digital recording of the session for the client is critical.

Detour: A Turning Point. Reflections from a Personal Journal

Morgan, 27, Insurance Business IT Analyst

"Since I am at a turning point in life and career right now, this is the perfect time for self-exploration.

"I know that I do not love what I am doing now, and I have taken steps such as going back to school to move toward my ultimate goals. But the transition, and knowing what steps to take, is not always the easiest thing in the world.

"I think it is interesting that there are certain things that you know about yourself and your work on some level, but you never really look at them. Like the patterns in your work style or the skills you really do have. Sometimes it is so hard for me to pinpoint the skills I currently have. You don't see them as skills or you overlook something because it's just something you do every day and you don't think of it as a skill. Concentrating on these things will really improve your career path and help you set realistic goals, which is important.

"It's also interesting to talk about social pressures and what is expected of us and what we think we should be doing because of what society says. For me, it's not family that puts these pressures on me, they are always very supportive of my choices. I think for me, the pressures come from myself, and the reason being is because I have these specific ideas of what I should be doing from society as a whole. Thinking about leaving my current job now and maybe taking a pay cut to get my foot in the door for something else is a hard choice for me.

"I have built up some time at my job, some decent pay, it's steady work, and all of these play a role. I think maybe I am crazy sometimes, but at the end of the day, I still realize that ultimately I do not like what I am doing, and maybe it's worth the change now to get to where I want to be long term. I have to look at the long-term picture."

* * *

TED'S RESULTS

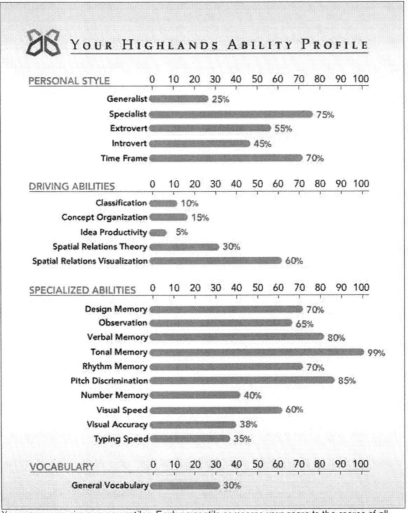

YOUR HIGHLANDS ABILITY PROFILE

PERSONAL STYLE — 0 10 20 30 40 50 60 70 80 90 100

- Generalist — 25%
- Specialist — 75%
- Extrovert — 55%
- Introvert — 45%
- Time Frame — 70%

DRIVING ABILITIES — 0 10 20 30 40 50 60 70 80 90 100

- Classification — 10%
- Concept Organization — 15%
- Idea Productivity — 5%
- Spatial Relations Theory — 30%
- Spatial Relations Visualization — 60%

SPECIALIZED ABILITIES — 0 10 20 30 40 50 60 70 80 90 100

- Design Memory — 70%
- Observation — 65%
- Verbal Memory — 80%
- Tonal Memory — 99%
- Rhythm Memory — 70%
- Pitch Discrimination — 85%
- Number Memory — 40%
- Visual Speed — 60%
- Visual Accuracy — 38%
- Typing Speed — 35%

VOCABULARY — 0 10 20 30 40 50 60 70 80 90 100

- General Vocabulary — 30%

Your scores are given as percentiles. Each percentile compares your score to the scores of all persons who have taken the same worksample.

"He flourishes in his strength."

— Homer, *The Odyssey*

"I never teach my pupils. I only attempt to provide the conditions in which they can learn."

— Albert Einstein

IV. Ted, 31, Director of Leadership Programs, Global Pharmaceutical Firm
Finding an Outlet for Creativity

This is a significant transition because, for the first time, many folks start to experience a real pull to focus on finding out what they really want to do and more important – if they are lucky – become more aware of how their strengths differ from those around them. Simultaneously, this period pulls even more for use of our creative powers regardless of whether we've been able to productively focus them until now.

OUR CONVERSATION

Ted, 31, was Director of Leadership Development Programs at a midsize global pharmaceutical firm. He had quit college and played in a rock band for several years, then got his degree in psychology. One of his college professors got him interested in organizational psychology. She also did consulting and Ted saw her as a role model.

Ted had always liked helping people understand things. He had tutored all through college. He said he loved "the moment when the light bulb goes on for people as they figure something out."

He had done some organizational development work at a small software company and also some private coaching as a consultant, but found he did not like the "selling" aspect of consulting work. In his current job, he worked in developing talent management and leadership programs, but coaching remained his passion. "If I could do that every day," he said, "that would be my dream job – to help executives work through their issues. The thing I feel that I'm a rock star at is when I am coaching. I've actually had to work harder on my project management skills and execution skills."

Ted's Grip score on the dynamometer came out about mid-range, which is generally a good result because it showed he could plow through frustration but at some point lift his head up and ask if a problem was worth the time and frustration it was causing.

People with low Grip can function well at work. They just need to learn how low their frustration tolerance can be with tasks that turn out to be more complex than originally gauged and they conserve their energy and take time to recuperate as well. And once you get to the main parts of the Ability Battery itself, there are no "good" results, certainly not where operating and learning styles are being measured rather than learned skills such as vocabulary size.

I then went through Ted's Ability Battery results with him, starting with work style.

On the Generalist/Specialist scale, he came out at 75th percentile **Specialist**, which put him at odds with the general population.

Generalists work well in large, bureaucratic organizations because they "think teamwork." They're built to almost automatically think that work is about working with and through others. They can be leaders, they can be followers. They thrive in environments where there's a lot happening simultaneously, where they can move between roles, work on teams, work with other people, where they become a jack-of-all-trades but not necessarily a master of any.

Specialists are driven by what goes on inside them. They are driven more by intensity and passion and they want to approach things by becoming experts. Specialists dive deep into an area of specialized knowledge or technique expertise and then emerge on the other side as "experts." It's not that they can't do these other things, it's just that they're really at their best when they're focused in that area of expertise.

I encourage people who test as "mid-range Specialists" to think of themselves as Specialists first and then as Generalists. Sometimes a person will spend the first part of their careers attaining expertise and then switch over to a managing role. It's just easier to make that transition, I told Ted, after they've acquired expertise and the confidence that goes with it. And frequently a Specialist will do better than a Generalist at managing a group of fellow Specialists.

Mastering an instrument is a solitary experience, and only when you have done that do you play in a band. It's not a group activity, initially.

"It's funny," said Ted. "Everybody thinks a band is that way and I explain to my wife, 'Yeah, I was the 10-year-old kid in my room that didn't come out playing the guitar, so everybody seems like they're so social, we're actually very introverted or we wouldn't be good at what we're good at."

In fact, on the Ability Battery, Ted tested as an **Extrovert**, although he felt that he had been more introverted when he was younger. I told him this was possible. I mentioned the pioneering work of British psychologist Hans Eysenck and his work on early formation of introversion and extroversion. His research suggests that perhaps instead of "changing," we consider that we might grow into ourselves as we grow older and as our environmental conditions change. Ted was now an Extroverted Specialist, someone who loves performing. And teaching is a type of performing.

It should be noted here that having abilities strongly geared in one direction doesn't preclude you from developing skills more commonly found in people with different abilities. It just takes more time and effort.

Studies by psychologist K. Anders Ericsson published in 2007 estimated that to become an expert in any complex field requires 10,000 hours of practice. The studies by Ericsson and his colleagues dealt with young violin players, chess players and others. As Malcolm Gladwell showed in his 2009 book *Outliers,* it applies in many

professions. Based on Ericsson's work, Gladwell concluded that be-
sides innate talent, a variety of factors, including **Family of Origin**,
determine who can become an expert.

Expert coaching can play a key role, not only in developing a new
skill but also in helping you determine where effort is likely to pay
off and where it isn't. A person with low **Pitch Discrimination** is
unlikely to ever become a symphony conductor.

A high potential leader client once asked me if he could become
a better leader of teams, given his reticent, analytical nature. Was
it even possible? Of course it is, I responded, if you play to your
strengths and become great at working with team members behind
the scenes first before having an open discussion among all members. Will you become the exuberant leader who fires up the team to
charge forward? Unlikely. At times, you could, of course, but not on
a routine basis.

In Ted's case, though, his **Introvert** and **Extrovert** scores were
fairly close. He was almost what we call an "ambivert," like someone
with dual citizenship or a switch hitter in baseball, who can hit from
both sides of the plate, although he may do better from one.

We next discussed Ted's **Time Frame** score, which was in the
70th percentile. Anything over the 64th percentile is considered
high, and this meant that Ted was comfortable thinking several years
ahead in planning strategy, either for his company or for himself.

People with low Time Frame, in contrast, are more comfortable
serving as "firemen," dealing with an immediate problem and then
moving on. IT troubleshooters would be a good example.

We then moved on to the **Driving Abilities**, the most basic abilities that almost always affect one's career choice or job performance.

Ted's **Classification** score was low, 10th percentile, and he was
concerned that this meant he wasn't good at problem-solving. I reassured him that this had nothing to do with his skill in solving problems, only with his method of doing so.

He simply was not a person who intuitively saw the answer to
a problem. He was more likely to think it through more carefully,

relying more on his own past experience – or input from co-workers – than his own gut instinct. This put him in fast company – CEOs, for example, tend to have low Classification scores. It makes them more patient and willing to listen to others.

With his low Classification score, would he have made a good emergency room physician? Well, it might have been difficult and were he inclined toward medicine, he might want to think of another specialty.

While management guru Peter Drucker is right in saying that we don't really *know* what we're good at, we do have an almost uncanny *sense* of it. My work with people – along with objective testing using timed work samples – is the best way of bringing that instinctive knowledge to the surface.

So for someone interested in coaching, low Classification made sense.

"If you're looking at developing people," I told him, "lower Classification is a better match. It's more about listening, more about being able to identify what abilities folks have.

When a person comes in with a problem, it's not about taking over the problem because you enjoy solving it. It's more about 'How do I develop this person so they can think about this for themselves?'"

I often use a sports analogy as a way to think of high and low percentiles when it comes to the Drivers in an attempt to clarify the differences. "Depending on the game you are playing, high and low scores mean different things. If you're playing basketball, then the high score wins. If you are playing golf, then it is the low scores that matter. Depending on how your percentiles stack up will determine what game you should be playing and knowing that makes all the difference. The difference is in how you use yourself.

"As you get older and have gathered experience in a role," I added, "low Classification looks different. You have a large enough store of experiences that you can .

Ted also had low scores in **Concept Organization** and **Idea Productivity**, which also fit into the profile of a more deliberate, experiential problem-solver.

I explained that someone with high Concept Organization "thinks in logical, engineer-like, methodical steps.

"People with high Concept Organization are extremely organized internally. They sit down and write something that doesn't require a lot of editing; it's just organized when it comes out. Lower Concept Organization, you're going to take more time and effort putting together a slide show."

People with high Idea Productivity, unlike Ted, "are people who are constantly brainstorming in their heads. They leave their boss's office and by the time they get to their own office, they've thought of 15 different ways to tackle the problem. Low Idea Productivity is about focus and follow-through."

I asked Ted – tongue in cheek, of course – "Who would you rather have doing brain surgery on you? Someone with low Idea Productivity or high Idea Productivity?"

"Low," he said.

"Exactly. You want someone who's skilled and trained…"

"Or not changing the procedure in the middle. Oh, I get it.

I do like to focus on one thing at a time."

Exactly what was shaping up for Ted was the profile of someone with an experiential problem-solving and decision-making style, i.e., using the past to solve current problems.

But he also had the ability to plan ahead for several years, be focused and decisive and follow through on decisions and plans.

Ted scored in the 30th percentile in **Spatial Relations Theory** and in the 60th percentile in **Spatial Relations Visualization**.

I told him that his theory score meant: "When there's a team that's facing a problem, being able to have face-to-face contact and interaction with them makes it a lot easier to understand what's going on and do something with them."

His Visualization score, on the other hand, showed some need to work with tangible objects.

Failure to use a strong Driving Ability is almost sure to bring frustration – it needs an outlet. But in some cases, that outlet can be outside one's job. In Ted's case, the outlet was three hobbies: playing musical instruments, floral design, and sometimes doing small home repairs.

"You hang a door," he said, "you know when it's hung, it's hung straight and it's true, and you get that sense that you don't get from the other work."

Ted's scores in several of the Specialized Abilities were high enough to constitute as a Driver along with low Classification, Concept Organization and Idea Productivity scores. Ted said it was natural that an accomplished musician like himself would score high in **Tonal Memory**. Actually, he had it backward: He probably became a successful musician because of his Tonal Memory abilities.

In the business world, Ted's Tonal Memory – the 99th percentile – would probably help him recall a conversation with a client from months earlier. His high **Design Memory** correlated with his skill and his passion in floral design.

He proudly showed me a colorful graphic he had created depicting a multi-layered talent management and succession planning system. The work clearly showed his abilities – high

Time Frame, high Design Memory, high **Pitch Discrimination** and being a Specialist.

He also had high scores in **Verbal Memory** and **Observation**, and the high Observation score was a good match with his low Idea Productivity. If both were high, he could have been – in his words – "all over the place."

Ted's creativity – expressed most obviously in his music – was a combination of Design Memory, Observation, Tonal Memory and Pitch Discrimination. And, of course, being a Specialist, with the tendency to think outside the box. And I noted that Idea Productivity alone has little to do with creativity. An author who writes a book every year is not necessarily more creative than one who writes one every four years.

The Ability Battery concludes with a test of **Vocabulary**, the one ability that can clearly be improved with study. Ted was in the upper end of the low range.

This is also the one ability in which a high score is clearly an advantage. It reflects your ability to communicate your thoughts and ideas to a wide range of people. It's not so much knowing and using big words as understanding the subtleties of words and the differences between them. Most of the business world is around low to mid-range. If there's a "classic" CEO profile, it's low Classification and Concept Organization, low Idea Productivity, high Time Frame and high Vocabulary.

TED'S DISCOVERIES

Ted needs to work on a plan that uses more of his considerable talents in the work setting. He should purposefully seek out roles in which he can hone his strength in long-term planning and use his creative abilities; for example, designing 3-D charts, brochures of where the organization is going. He should also play to his strengths in developing others and last, work out how people on his team contribute differently and maximize how he deploys them.

As the session ended and I reviewed Ted's scores again with him, I expressed concern that he might need to find more creative outlets in his work in addition to his music. This could mean more emphasis on coaching, or perhaps getting on planning committees where his high Time Frame would be rewarding to him and useful to the company.

"When you're young," I told him, "you think you can bypass your natural strengths and limits because there's energy and time for everything. Then, when you're in your 30s, you start to think, 'Now I want to do what I'm really good at.'

"At this point in your career, you might intuitively know what you can contribute and what you're good at and how you are different from others. We have now made your strengths more objective, put some labels on your behavior that hopefully allow you to articulate your strengths easier. Now it is about making a plan to move in that direction."

Takeaways

- Having abilities strongly geared in one direction doesn't preclude you from developing skills more commonly found in people with different abilities. It just takes more time and effort.
- Failure to use a strong Driving Ability is almost sure to bring frustration.
- As we get older, we "grow into ourselves, our abilities."

CHRIS'S RESULTS

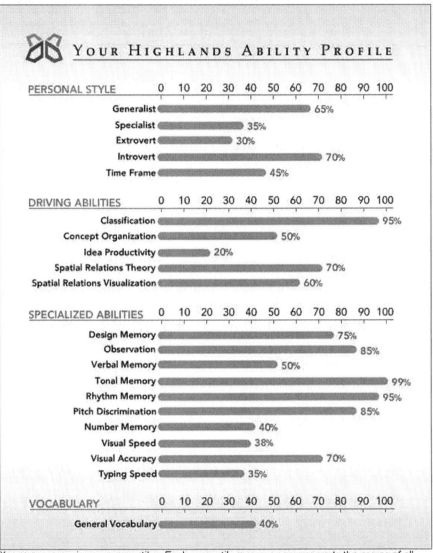

YOUR HIGHLANDS ABILITY PROFILE

PERSONAL STYLE — 0 10 20 30 40 50 60 70 80 90 100

- Generalist — 65%
- Specialist — 35%
- Extrovert — 30%
- Introvert — 70%
- Time Frame — 45%

DRIVING ABILITIES — 0 10 20 30 40 50 60 70 80 90 100

- Classification — 95%
- Concept Organization — 50%
- Idea Productivity — 20%
- Spatial Relations Theory — 70%
- Spatial Relations Visualization — 60%

SPECIALIZED ABILITIES — 0 10 20 30 40 50 60 70 80 90 100

- Design Memory — 75%
- Observation — 85%
- Verbal Memory — 50%
- Tonal Memory — 99%
- Rhythm Memory — 95%
- Pitch Discrimination — 85%
- Number Memory — 40%
- Visual Speed — 38%
- Visual Accuracy — 70%
- Typing Speed — 35%

VOCABULARY — 0 10 20 30 40 50 60 70 80 90 100

- General Vocabulary — 40%

Your scores are given as percentiles. Each percentile compares your score to the scores of all persons who have taken the same worksample.

"We all grow up with the weight of history on us. Our ancestors dwell in the attics of our brains as they do in the spiraling chains of knowledge hidden in every cell of our bodies."
— Shirley Abbott

"Things do not change; we change."
— Henry David Thoreau

The Annotated Walden (1970)

V. Chris, 36, Graphic Designer
Rethinking at 36

Here is a person still early in his career who is considering what on the surface might be considered a significant departure but in reality may be an elaboration! More important, here is a person interested in looking at his career but not feeling much pressure from within. Likely this is because he was in that period we call a Building Stage, a relative calm between the Turning Point turbulence. In the Building Stage, a person has accepted a view and a role, an identity of who he is in the work setting, and he works at forging skills that will enhance his competence.

Additionally Chris, like 30% of my clients, had grown up in Philadelphia, where – as in most of the country – folks usually stayed with one company for 30 years, such as Maytag in Iowa. That didn't leave much room for many role models for career change. Additionally, folks don't consider how they are affected over time by the Family of Origin and preceding generations.

There may have been, say, an uncle who was deemed eccentric because he defied family tradition and moved to California to open a business. Maybe he became a model to draw from as one contemplated change. In a sense, we are always working with the Family of

Origin images and other systems that have a gravitational pull on our choices, as the accompanying family of origin breakout note from another client in his 30s shows.(Page 73)

OUR CONVERSATION

Chris was going on 36, a graphic designer in the branding and creative services department of a communications company. His job was part of the corporate communications department. He did posters, pamphlets, brochures and other materials. He was also working on the company's new Web site and expected to work the following year on redesigning its outdated Intranet.

He had been with the company for eight years.

"And what is something you do in this job that comes easy to you, is fun, is almost stressless?" I asked.

"I think it comes down more to the subject matter than to the projects themselves," he said. "I'm doing a brochure right now for the planning department about product lines. We've done it before, and it's an update of two years ago. The group is one or two people and they're easy to work with and the material is familiar. They give us a lot of leeway on it."

"So take me to the other side," I said. "What's a task or a role that takes more time and energy?"

"Well, sometimes we're called on to illustrate concepts that don't necessarily lend themselves to a visual identity. From time to time people ask us for a graphic that represents our markets, and it's way too complex to illustrate in a single graphic or a single piece of art. So I sit there with a blank stare and no real ideas.

"Then there are some groups that know what they want and don't really give you the freedom to show your creativity. So that makes the project a lot harder because you have an internal struggle about whether to tell them it's not going to look correct. I pride myself on new ideas, fresh ideas."

Chris had thought about going into the Air Force and had applied unsuccessfully to the Air Force Academy. He also thought about aeronautical engineering but realized that his real passion for what was then the brand-new field of computer animation. He went to a university to study in the field "and really kind of never looked back."

Can you guess what I would ask him next? "So when you look ahead five years," I asked him, "what do you see yourself doing?"

"Well, I've become much more interested in the engineering side of our business. But math has always been a struggle for me. Writing has always come more easily."

On the Ability Battery, Chris scored in the 68th percentile as a **Generalist** and also tested as an **Introvert**. "It's not that Introverts don't like people," I said, "it's that they go inside and think things through before they say them. It's being more comfortable with structured interactions rather than freewheeling discussions. The opposite example would be someone like Joe Biden, who thinks out loud, basically."

"Yes," he said. "When I'm designing something, I kind of hide it until it's almost time to present it. Some people say, 'Oh, look,' when they're just at the beginning stage. I want it to be complete before I talk about it.

"When it comes to social activity, I think I have what you could almost consider a warm-up time, where I'm not really one to go out and meet people or talk to people first, but if I'm introduced to them, then I have no problem interacting."

I told him his results were interesting in that, more often than not, Generalists tended to be extroverted. "So you can be described as a team player who wants to work with other people and embraces that, and at the same time wants to have their own distance and be detached to have their own thoughts.

"As a manager, you would be team-oriented, but when you went back to your office and thought about what the team had decided, you might be detached enough to reach a different conclusion. Extroverted Generalists can be too connected to the emotional climate Chris was mid-range on **Time Frame,** giving him some flexibility in terms of planning. "Low Time Frame people want projects six months, nine months, 12 months maximum," I said. "The mid-range folks like yourself are able to go either way, but most of the time they want to look at the fire and say, 'OK, we can put it out, but how can we prevent it from reoccurring?' That's going out a little longer, maybe one to three years."

In **Classification**, Chris was in the 95th percentile. "This is super fast, like a trial attorney or an emergency room physician," I told him. "Other people don't know how you got there sometimes."

This resonated with Chris. He said he sometimes interviewed candidates for his department, and "after five minutes, I'm just going through the motions because I've already made my decision."

He scored mid-range in **Concept Organization**, the more methodical, slower-paced way of solving problems through deductive reasoning rather than the inductive reasoning of Classification. "Mid-range means you've got enough structure going on in your head that you can organize yourself OK," I said. "You don't need a time management seminar." I added that it was Concept Organization that helps you explain to others how you solved a problem.

In **Idea Productivity**, Chris scored fairly low (20th percentile), which he found logical. "I've felt that I had a filter in my head, like I don't want to type things that are nonsensical or off the wall. I focus on the more realistic, concrete-type ideas and concepts."

Chris scored in the 70th percentile in **Spatial Relations Theory**, high enough that he could grasp higher-level math despite his stated problems with the subject.

"I noticed in the report that it mentions artistic creations, too," he said.

"Yes, exactly, being able to design something."

As I listened to Chris during this feedback session, I realized that a major sub-theme in this discussion was his virtual disbelief of his own abilities. Chris didn't see himself as anything but ordinary. For him, reviewing these results illuminated his significant potential.

I asked Chris about his interests outside work, since these also help round out the picture of someone's skills and abilities, both what he likes doing and what he does well.

He told me he played several sports – hockey and mountain biking – and liked to cook and work with computers. He liked making figures out of modeling clay with his son and said he would do more home repair projects if he had the time.

His **Spatial Relations Visualization** score was in the 60th percentile, which explained his ability to fix computers and play sports – both hands-on activities – not to mention cooking.

His **Design Memory** was in the 75th percentile: "You see a picture and it sticks in your head. You see a design, you see someone on a Web site and you see a picture there and it sticks." I added that high scores in this area often correlate with wanting to experience tangible outcomes in a project. His 85th percentile score in **Observation** clearly made him able to read situations easily in both the office environment and a basketball court. "I am referring to your being able to read body language that allows you to pick up on feints and direction changes when guarding a player."

His **Verbal Memory** was mid-range in the 50th percentile, but his **Tonal Memory** score, 99th percentile, meant he would rely on listening rather than reading to absorb material whenever possible. His **Rhythm Memory** was in the 95th percentile, accounting for his ability to learn through movement to master sports. "But it's also about learning through movement," I said, "so you learn by writing things. If you're taking notes, you don't have to read those notes again. It's just that the very act of taking notes is another way for you to take information in."

CHRIS' DISCOVERIES

Chris possesses multiple ways of taking in new information. He is a quick learner. He has strong abilities in conceptualizing and designing images. He is also quite creative, and the quality of what he produces art-wise will be high. He just isn't coming up with lots of ideas in a short period of time. I also recommended that during his workday, he find ways to get up and move around occasionally: "You could probably be more productive because "If you move just because that Rhythm Memory is at a physical level, it needs expression. It's like people who have to play the drums. They have to get it out of their system. If you can get up and move around, it clears the cobwebs for you. Just sitting behind a desk all day looking at a computer screen doesn't work for you."

This is a big first step for Chris as he begins to think through his needs and goals and then goes to work on thinking through his next steps. For instance, getting an M.B.A. might not be the best solution because it still may leave his strong Spatial Relations abilities out of the picture. On the other hand, an M.B.A. could be a confidence builder for someone who never saw himself as a student but clearly possesses. Moreover, the M.B.A. would be a way to tap into his Generalist/Introvert personal style and more easily move into his thinking of himself eventually leading/managing a small team of designers or technical professionals.

Takeaways

- **For You:** Being low in Idea Productivity doesn't equal being unartistic.
- **For teams:** Extroverted Generalist managers can get so absorbed in the emotional climate of the group and team harmony that they have trouble getting the distance to make a difficult decision.
- **For coaches:** In explaining skills and abilities, interests outside work can sometimes shed as much light as experiences on the job. Interests can add balance and creativity to one's life.

Detour - Family of Origin. Reflections of Bob, a client in his early 30's.

"One of the things that I was thinking about once we ended today's workshop is that it can be very easy to slip into a system's goal rather than my own.

"I've come to realize a very focused personal development strategy. I've begun to see how well ingrained systems are in my decision-making process. It's been a little painful and relieving to look at my past decisions. This is not to say that I don't take personal responsibility for my decisions, but it's interesting to see that pattern of influence that has followed me for so many years.

"The pain comes from making mistakes that have a lasting impact. For example, as I reflect on why I left the Armed Forces, many of the finalizing decisions came from my perception of the systems I was/am in. I never really thought what I was doing deserved any special attention; I felt like I was just doing my job.

"On the other hand, the relief comes from being able to step back and see what contributed to my decision(s). This class is giving me the vision to see things from a different perspective. Stepping outside my systems and looking within gives me the vantage point to see a big decision, how I responded, and what influences were present and how I reacted to them. That is valuable to me.

"While I look at these decisions, I can also see how my innate characteristics have helped and hindered my development. Understanding that my talents are not necessarily an advantage has been something in the back of my mind for some time but (now I'm) bringing them forward for a more thorough analysis. I can see the value in building myself based on talents but consideration must be given to how those talents can work against me if not harnessed appropriately."

* * *

MARTHA'S RESULTS

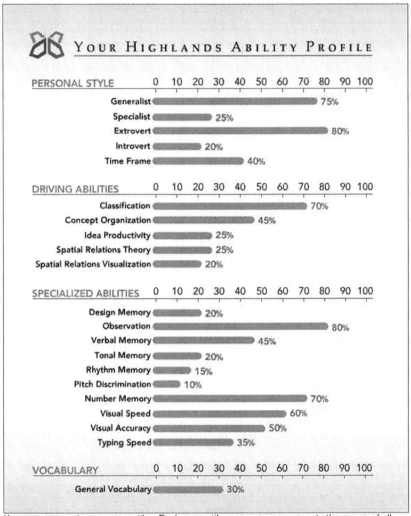

Your scores are given as percentiles. Each percentile compares your score to the scores of all persons who have taken the same worksample.

"My wife and I went to purchase a new mattress. As we did the requisite lying down on it to get the feel, our salesperson asked me if I had considered a California King size bed. In my head, I thought he was trying to move me into an even more expensive bed, but I quickly realized he was staring at my feet as they were hanging over the bed from my ankles down. Sir, he said, California King doesn't cost more, it just adds 3-4 inches lengthwise. That night I went home and noticed how I slept on my bed. I lay in different ways, but only at an angle or in the fetal position did my feet stay on the bed. I thought and thought and saw how I had adapted to the bed size. Not knowing what was possible or what options I had I had adapted myself to something that didn't fit. In the a.m., I called and ordered a California King!"

– The proverb of the mattress

VI. Martha, 39, Senior IT Project Manager
Developing a Vision

We may experience the "dreaded 30s assessment," as one client recently referred to it, and take advantage of the crisis to come up with a vision. More often than not, we stumble forward, searching externally for the right situation. We are all looking for ways to make it. We seize on an aspect of a new situation or career and then figure we can adapt until the fit over time becomes clearly uncomfortable. As we head into our late 30s and yet another Turning Point looms, we see the consequences of choosing, even if one doesn't choose. In an earlier book, we described this as the stress cycle. Without the time to reflect and reevaluate that apparently the Turning Points in a career can provide, we may end up doing the same thing over and over.

OUR CONVERSATION

At the time of our session, Martha was Senior IT Project Manager for a large financial services company, one of a series of jobs she had held over the past few years.

She was frustrated at the lack of a pattern in her career. And it soon became apparent that the problem was neither a lack of ability nor an unwillingness to work hard. She just had not developed an overarching Personal Vision.

"I feel like I haven't put a lot of effort in finding jobs," she said. "They sort of have come to me, and not as quickly as I would like them to. It sort of feels like, OK, well, this was all that was available and that's what I'm taking. I wasn't very strategic in my thought process."

She had studied marketing in college with a double major in accounting, and graduated in 1986 in a tough economy. After taking a sales job recommended by a family member and not liking it, she moved to a housewares manufacturing company and took a marketing job.

After working a series of part-time jobs for a year, she took a sales job and once again saw it eliminated when a new manager came in. She did not receive mentoring in any of her jobs. Then she took a sales job that was a mismatch for her skills.

"I think the person that hired me thought I was more analytical and I'm more 'communications' and creative," she said.

Martha went back to school for a couple of years, had her second child and went back to a sales job at a furniture company for which she had worked earlier. She then moved on to a food industry sales job and was again laid off.

"I see this pattern, and this is the third time I've been laid off," she said. "Maybe I was a victim of circumstances, or maybe someone is telling me I'm not in the right field. I don't know."

Martha was 39 and clearly at one of the Turning Points that regularly occur in our work lives. "In 10 years," she said, "I'm not going to be able to be making major job changes." I disagreed and told her so, but it was obvious that she really needed to identify her strengths and find ways to play to them.

We started with the Grip test, and her score came out extremely high. This indicated a good amount of natural persistence. But people with high Grip scores often don't sit back and evaluate where they are in a particular job or in their career. They just keep going and going, Energizer Bunny-style.

I asked her to look back on her career and think of something where "you were firing on all cylinders when you were in it, and what was it that you did?" (For a brief exercise about how to use your recall of these moments, see the Test Drives section at the end of the book.)

She named working as a consultant setting up trade shows. "I had free rein to basically do anything I wanted to because even though I didn't have anybody guiding me, I could quickly analyze the situation and see where there were problems and put my energy into solving those problems and see quick results." But the job also became routine and boring after a while. She also didn't like the fact that between shows, her work was done almost entirely on the phone. Perhaps key to her current dissatisfaction?

"I would see the fantastic completion and that was a real big high when I was on site," she said. "And when the event was over, it was a big letdown."

I asked her what roles she saw herself in.

"Well, I think I need to push myself to be in more of a leading role or managerial role," she said. "I tend to be a little shy when it comes to public speaking and standing out. I need to push myself because I know I have it in me."

Martha ended up in the extreme Generalist side of the Generalist/Specialist scale, and I told her that people who are Generalists should consider themselves as people who can easily work through others to get things done.

"You can think of this as marketing, leading people who are themselves marketing experts," I said. "Your contribution in that is leadership and working the team dynamics. Your power is that solid footing in the Generalist world that makes it easier to persuade and influence and be aware of the group dynamics or the team dynamics."

On the Extrovert/Introvert scale, Martha came out strongly as an Extrovert, which clearly explained why she was so frustrated with a job that was done mostly on the phone.

"People who are high on the extroversion side are people who get energy from other people," I told her. "They want to talk things out, get exchanges, get ideas going. People who are in the Introvert world want to think about what they're doing, prefer to engage in structured interaction, keeping it small, keep it limited.

"With you, talking about it makes it real. You put the words out there and as you see the words come out of your mouth, you get the sense, 'Oh, that's real.' The extroverted world is a real energy boost."

I could clearly see her in a role where she was leading others, "rallying them around a vision, getting them excited, getting them on the same page and then persuading them." I sensed she hadn't had this level of passion for anything she had done.

Martha had been thinking about owning her own business, which could have fit her profile. So did her mid-range score on Time Frame. She could comfortably think about three years ahead, sufficient to establish a business plan. Interestingly, she had stayed in most of her previous jobs between two and four years.

Martha's Classification score was in the 70th percentile, and this was clearly an ability she had to use. "You see an outline of a problem and you immediately jump to a solution," I told her. "People are wondering, 'How did she get there?'

"The person with high Classification thrives in a fast-paced environment with lots of new problems coming at them all the time. Once a problem has been solved, a person with high Classification really couldn't care about solving it again. They're looking for novelty, ambiguity. Think trial attorneys, think physicians in the emergency room, think about consultants who are asked to come in and fix a problem and diagnose it. That kind of environment."

High Classification also has its downside. As I explained to her, it can come off as arrogance, and if the person stays with the situation too long, she can in effect create more problems just so she can solve them. Also, "they can be pretty impatient in terms of other people's development. They have a harder time listening."

They also tend to have problems delegating. Difficulty in delegating can be a drawback in a large corporation but is well suited to entrepreneurial roles. It can also lead to procrastination as you keep picking apart the solutions you have found.

Interestingly, leading executive coach Marshall Goldsmith titled his recent book *What Got You Here Won't Get You There* –and what is essentially described by that title can be the dilemma of the high Classification people, i.e., rising to a certain level based on their abilities to be fast problem-solvers, until that very talent hinders them in large organizations.

To sum it up, it's great in an entrepreneur, but it can become an Achilles' heel once the business gets bigger and processes need to be put in place.

In Concept Organization, Martha scored in the 45th percentile, mid-range. If a problem was going to require step-by-step, deductive reasoning, she would probably take longer to solve it.

"This may not be a big strength, but it's not going to be a big challenge, either," I told her. "You can be organized, you can kind of put things together. But you may not want to have that as the big part of your role when you're doing project management all the time, for instance."

Martha had a low score in Idea Productivity, and as I always do in such cases, I reassured her that this had nothing to do with the quality of her ideas. "It's kind of like you can fill a bathtub by turning the faucet on high or you can drip the water into the tub. It still gets full."

Similarly, a teacher high in Idea Productivity might come up with different ways to say the same thing to a struggling student while one with high Classification – like Martha – would be more likely to explain how the student got the wrong answer. In the end, both could help the student with the problem as long as the teacher with high Classification did not become impatient.

As I explained, being an Extrovert could combine well with being low in Idea Productivity because she would be comfortable interacting with other people to get their ideas. "If you think about being an entrepreneur," I said, "it's about being able to stay focused on the vision and mission of your company, not to be distracted by saying that 'Today we're going left, then go home and have some new ideas and then you tell everybody, 'Now we're going right today.'"

I told her about a consultant I knew who had his own business where he was surrounded by Introvert/Specialists who – unbeknownst to him – were low Idea Productivity. They were great at their jobs but totally lost in staff meetings where the consultant wanted to brainstorm about challenges or think out of the box.

The Ability Battery opened the consultant's mind to the diversity of styles and also his need to add some new blood to his company.

Martha scored low in both measures of Spatial Relations. This showed her as comfortable in the world of abstractions and ideas, with no need to derive satisfaction from dealing with the physical world in terms of either design or hands-on work.

"It's about people who manage other people, CEOs," I told her. "It's about trainers, it's about salespeople, it's about lawyers and accountants."

Martha also scored low in Design Memory and Tonal Memory but high in Observation. "People of high Observation are people who are extremely aware of and attendant to visual stimuli," I told her. "You walk into someone's office and you're aware that the last time you were there the picture was on the other wall. I mean that's hitting you all the time and it's like you can't turn it off.

"It's also being aware of what people are saying nonverbally, being able to observe the things they're not saying as they're speaking to you."

Her Verbal Memory was mid-range, 45th percentile. This ability is about remembering what you read, and since reading is one of the two main ways we take in information, Martha needed to think of ways to compensate for a mid-range ability, such as high-lighting key words or phrases, taking notes or even reading aloud to herself.

In some parts of her life, she was already doing it. She said that just writing a grocery list helped her remember what to get at the market even when she forgot to bring the list.

Martha also scored low in Pitch Discrimination and Rhythm Memory but high in Number Memory. I reassured her that her high Grip score showed a persistence that would compensate for low scores in several of the Learning Channels' abilities.

Rhythm Memory is basically learning through doing. She was not surprised at her low score because she had found it frustrating to go to gym classes such as kickboxing: "But I keep at it until I get it right." Her high Grip was coming through again, a reminder that persistence is often an asset but that it sometimes keeps you from playing to your strengths.

My own Rhythm Memory, or muscle memory, score is low. "Every time I swing the golf club, it is like a new event. Who knows what I'm doing," I said. "It's like going to get ballroom dancing lessons. That is painful. I tried. My wife as well as the instructor have high Rhythm Memory!"

But Martha also scored high – 70th percentile – on Number Memory. A high score in this ability comes in handy in some virtually useless areas – remembering many phone numbers when you own a PDA – and some very useful ones, like budgeting.

"Given the reality of today's corporate environment, it's particularly useful for women in executive roles to have high Number Memory," I told her. "They're not intimidated by numbers." However, having low Number Memory requires one to find ways to compensate, such as taking careful notes or even bringing "numbers people" to meetings.

I told her that most likely we all have compensated in some fashion for low abilities, like an executive with low Number Memory bringing her "numbers people" to a meeting or a note-taker whose memory is improved by the act of writing things down.

Martha said, "I find that in jobs where I was responsible for putting together budgets, that would be the last task I would take on. I procrastinate on that particular task. To me, that's mundane."

So her resistance to budgeting turned out to have no relationship to her comfort – or lack of it – with numbers.

"People who procrastinate when they're high in Classification often want to," I told her. "They see it as such a mundane activity. It's not particularly interesting, complex and novel. If they leave it until towards the end, they'll at least get an adrenaline charge out of doing it to that point."

This was one more illustration of how hard it really can be to recognize our strengths and to get others to recognize them. People around us can tend to define us in terms of the one ability they see most. Our job is to be able to articulate what we have to offer and market ourselves accordingly.

"So it wasn't necessarily the numbers in the task," I told her. "It was a task that was kind of repetitive and not particularly a new problem."

"Well, if it's something I own, I'll create those challenges," she said. The entrepreneurial piece again comes to the surface.

Then came a real eye-opener – Vocabulary. Martha's was in the 30th percentile, which was not that unusual. A typical score for someone in the business world is in the 25th to 40th percentile. But it becomes a challenge when dealing with CEOs or other people with higher scores: The benefit of a higher Vocabulary is purely being able to develop a rapport with a wider range of people as well as having a well-differentiated way of articulating your thoughts to others.

Martha had said earlier in the session that she rarely had a problem coming up with a solution to a problem but sometimes had trouble explaining it. This was the key. "I often times will pause mid-sentence because I can't think of the right word to say," she said now.

I told her that the discrepancy between her high Classification score and much lower Vocabulary score could be a source of frustration if she didn't work on the latter. I recommended use of the Web site http://www.wordsmart.com as a start.

MARTHA'S DISCOVERIES

Becoming clear about how her strong Extroversion, high Classification and low Idea Productivity worked together coupled with her tenacity seemed like a light bulb going off for Martha. Suddenly her dream of a entrepreneurial role didn't seem so pie in the sky!

We reviewed and summarized the test results again and talked about the general characteristics of any new job that could be a good match.

Her Extrovert/Generalist profile made her a good match for marketing jobs, and I told her that some of those might not have worked out because "they had a more Specialist role and you didn't take into consideration the fit between your work style and the environment.

"The key is looking at what are the activities you'll be doing. Are there going to be enough problems for you to solve? That's the key. Are you going to be able to work with people on a regular basis that's a high energy place? Are you going to come in and be seen as someone who knows a lot about a variety of industries?

"I think these are the biggest ones, and not being in a role where you have to generate lots of ideas on a short-term basis.

"You're determined. That's one of your biggest selling points. You can say, 'No matter what it takes, I'll just do it.'"

Takeaways

- **For your team:** Having low Number Memory requires one to find ways to compensate, such as taking careful notes or even bringing "numbers people" to meetings.
- **For you:** If you are low in Verbal Memory, you can compensate by using your other, better working Learning Channels: If it is Rhythm Memory, then write questions to yourself on what you read, or if higher in Tonal Memory, try reading aloud to yourself. But remember that being low in a Learning Channel doesn't mean you can't, it is more about needing to give yourself time.

- **For you:** People can tend to define us in terms of the one ability they see most or what they need. Our job is to be able to articulate what we have to offer and market ourselves.

SAMANTHA'S RESULTS

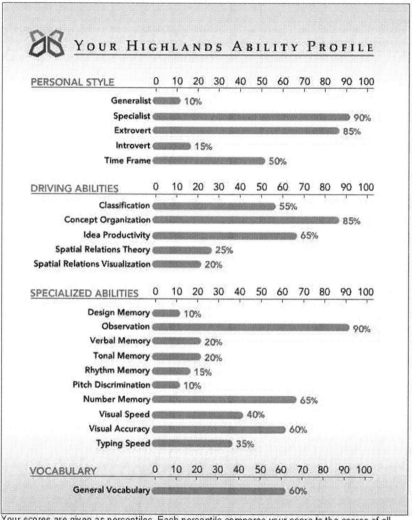

Your scores are given as percentiles. Each percentile compares your score to the scores of all persons who have taken the same worksample.

"You know the Greeks didn't write obituaries, they only asked one question after a man died: Did he have passion?"

— Dean Kansky (Jeremy Piven)
in the movie Serendipity (2001)

VII. Samantha, 40, Director of Sales Support
Puzzle, Passion, and the Need for People Interaction

Midlife is a time of great challenges and choices. In either case, there is no denying the significant changes going on within us and around us. Passion that has not been channeled and expressed into constructive and productive outlets creates discomfort within us. We can delay our expression as we often need to stay focused on the daily routine – house, family, mortgage, other needs that must be met. Bubbling underneath are passions, those parts of ourselves that need to be figured out and used in society. The dilemma at this Turning Point, I believe, is magnified for the person with a Specialist orientation.

OUR CONVERSATION

Samantha, 40, was Director of Sales Support for a major pharmaceutical company with which she had spent virtually her entire adult career. When I worked with her, she had six people on her team.

"I started out as an office-based sales rep and that role was very easy," she said. "I was managing a territory, conducting the business planning, working with two other team members. We took a sales territory that had been near the bottom and turned it around to be one of their top 10 nationally.

"I then got promoted to a hospital rep position, calling on an academic medical center and large community hospital, using the same selling skills but also calling on major opinion leaders. I had a few more management responsibilities but became frustrated because it was the type of job where it was difficult to measure success. I was calling on just a couple of accounts and customer bases.

"I then moved into the regional sales office, training new hires and doing the first round of interviews for district sales managers. I had a really good gut instinct for who would turn out to be a top producer. I also took on a rotational assignment that pretty much had me writing policy and I didn't really care for that. I didn't find it very exciting or challenging."

Samantha had her bachelor's degree in health care information. "My father and mother had been in pharmaceutical sales, so I had grown up with it," she said.

I asked her what role she saw for herself in the future: "What would you like to be doing five years from now?"

"Well, that's a challenging question for me because I've been trying to figure that out, not get caught into the success or financials of where I'm at.

"I like politics. I like the whole political campaign process." Samantha had done a 21-month rotation in Washington, D.C., to work on a project on childhood obesity.

"I did a lot of market research, putting a plan together. If our company were to get involved, what would that look like, what would the cost be, what would be the time investment? We wanted to make a national presence. We started reaching out to nonprofit foundations, academic centers, arranging interviews with experts. That work I really enjoyed.

"I could see myself doing advocacy work, pushing a cause and being very energized by that, or working on a politician's campaign, somebody I had a belief in.

"If I stay with this company, I really struggle because marketing isn't adventurous to me. I don't know enough about R&D to say yes or no. I need something with a lot of people interaction. I miss that from my sales days."

Samantha was strongly into the Specialist camp, with an 82nd percentile score, a pretty strong finding.

"Well, that's why I feel different a lot of the times."

"Specialists tend to feel different because they don't run with the crowd," I told her. "If they try to be like everybody else, they feel out of sorts with themselves."

Samantha also ranked high on the scale as an Extrovert, someone who plugs into the interpersonal world when under stress. "Extroversion and Specialists are a unique combination and that's the performing personality."

"That must be why my sister keeps saying that she can see me as a motivational speaker."

"Well, that is the personality type. It's about getting energy from others."

In Time Frame, Samantha was mid-range – 50th percentile – giving her the ability to do long-term strategic planning or concentrate on short-term results. She said she was much happier in a place where she can be involved in strategy. The childhood obesity project, for example, eating disorder project, for example, had a five-year time line.

"OK, there you go," I said. "Three to five years is good. It's in your comfort zone."

Samantha found this particularly meaningful in terms of sales. In some cases, she said, a sales unit might be thinking only one year ahead. But increasing sales in one year, she noted, is not helpful if it means they will decline in the following year.

I agreed: "They just need someone like you to help them stretch out, to see things in a series of 12-month increments so they can get to three years."

Samantha scored fairly high in Classification, 55th percentile, and I gave her the usual psychological Miranda warning about high Classification people coming off as arrogant to co-workers who don't size up problems as quickly.

"There's a certain criticalness. ...It's critical in the sense that it finds flaws in systems, that's just the nature of the ability. And it becomes critical of other people."

She scored much higher, 85th percentile, in Concept Organization. Overall, her results were indicative of what I call a "consultative problem-solving decision-making style...which is about you being asked to come in as an expert, a Specialist, to come in and solve a problem and you diagnose it using your Classification and then you use Concept Organization to tell people how they need to approach it so they can solve it."

This hit home with her. "When I was a regional analyst, I was basically an adviser to the regional vice president. 'You have an issue in the Chicago market, here's what it is, here's what we need to do to fix it.' If I can do that I'm as happy as the day is long."

"Right. Consider the times when you feel you've been at your peak in terms of productivity, being satisfied, working relatively stress-free. Usually that happens when people are using their abilities. So you can break down that experience and look at what abilities you were using and how do I replicate that."

This type of exchange where a dialogue emerges is key to adapting the Battery results! Folks aren't necessarily being told anything they don't know. Vague notions and ideas are sharpened until they break through the surface of old thought patterns and lead to the clients' heightened understanding of themselves.

Samantha's experiences were also typical of someone with high Idea Productivity, which she also had.

"Being able to persuade and influence is high Idea Productivity," I told her. "Generating ideas, being able to think on your feet, coming up with alternative ways, coming up with analogies, metaphors to describe and overcome resistance and get your point across."

She said that some parts of her job seemed unusually stressful, although she got them done.

"That means there's some mismatch with your abilities," I said. "That's going to be something for you to identify." But it was also something for her to consider when choosing with whom to work.

"I don't know who's on your team," I said, "but it's always interesting to think of how they complement you. I mean, is there somebody on the team who has low Idea Productivity? Is there someone with low Concept Organization, who's more likely to say, 'OK, we've talked about and analyzed this enough, let's move on it now'?"

We then discussed Samantha's Specialized Abilities, and what struck me here was her high Observation, which combined with high Concept Organization to give her what I call the "investigative profile."

"I guess that would explain why as a child, or even now, I love reading mystery novels," she said.

"Yes, and that's in your work when you think about it," I said. "You're looking for patterns. I sensed that when you were talking about the childhood obesity project in terms of the variety of people you were talking to and the stuff you were pulling together from different sources. There was a puzzle you were trying to fix or solve."

"Yes, that would be an accurate description." More often than not, our childhood fascinations are clues to future work roles.

Among the Learning Channels, Samantha was high only in Number Memory, 65th percentile.

"How do you compensate for lower Learning Channels?" I asked. "You put them together. When you need to learn something fast, the way to reduce the stress of it is not to rely on just one modality but kind of read it, read it out loud, write stuff about it, draw a picture or draw a concept of it and – most importantly, I think – talk about it with someone else and then kind of pose yourself problems about it."

"It takes me down memory lane," she said. "I'm just thinking about when I was in college or even when I was taking this test (the Ability Battery). I know things were going fast. I was trying to read certain things out loud so that I would remember them.

"Reading out loud, organizing and analyzing the information to be learned, and – most important – using multiple channels are all ways for you to learn new information quickly. You've made some compensation unconsciously already in terms of how you learn. I'm talking about being more conscious, purposeful and articulate about it."

SAMANTHA'S DISCOVERIES

The three high Drivers for Samantha – Classification, Concept Organization and Idea Productivity – all need to be used. Note the roles in which she felt energized as a result of frequent use of these Drivers. Combined with the passion of a Specialist and need for people interaction (extroversion) as well as high Observation, they make for a strong pull to roles in which she becomes an expert, studying patterns, drawing together pieces of a puzzle and communicating through her interaction. Leading a small team of other Specialists would be a key to thinking of her future role as a leader.

Samantha needs and wants to decide after reflection, research and informational interviews what idea she wants to put her passion behind and then to make sure the role provides her avenues for expression of all her powerful Drivers!

In the midlife Turning Point, we are faced with life and career decisions just as in the previous ones. Professional opportunities may be greater, but they won't last forever.

So now the stakes are higher!

Takeaways

- **For you:** Passion not channeled into constructive outlets usually leads to frustration.
- **For you:** If you have lower Learning Channels, reduce stress by trying to absorb material in different ways (look at your other abilities) – read it aloud, draw a picture or concept of it, talk it over with someone else.
- **For coaches:** While some of the profiles presented appear to have similar Personal Styles (Specialist/Extrovert), one really needs to focus on the Drivers as well to assist folks in seeing their uniqueness.

DENNIS'S RESULTS

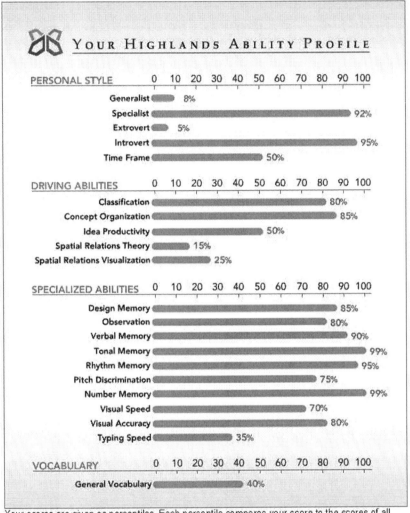

YOUR HIGHLANDS ABILITY PROFILE

PERSONAL STYLE
0 10 20 30 40 50 60 70 80 90 100

- Generalist 8%
- Specialist 92%
- Extrovert 5%
- Introvert 95%
- Time Frame 50%

DRIVING ABILITIES
0 10 20 30 40 50 60 70 80 90 100

- Classification 80%
- Concept Organization 85%
- Idea Productivity 50%
- Spatial Relations Theory 15%
- Spatial Relations Visualization 25%

SPECIALIZED ABILITIES
0 10 20 30 40 50 60 70 80 90 100

- Design Memory 85%
- Observation 80%
- Verbal Memory 90%
- Tonal Memory 99%
- Rhythm Memory 95%
- Pitch Discrimination 75%
- Number Memory 99%
- Visual Speed 70%
- Visual Accuracy 80%
- Typing Speed 35%

VOCABULARY
0 10 20 30 40 50 60 70 80 90 100

- General Vocabulary 40%

Your scores are given as percentiles. Each percentile compares your score to the scores of all persons who have taken the same worksample.

"In the middle of the journey...I came to myself in a dark wood."

– Dante, The Inferno

"I knew I was going to take the wrong train, so I left early"

– Yogi Berra

VIII. Dennis, 41, IT Project Manager
At the Midlife Transition

For many of us, jobs and then careers can happen by a combination of accident and luck. For instance, if I hadn't been dragged to a lecture by a psychology professor at one of the universities to which I was applying, we may not have met and talked, and I would never have heard her reaching out to me about my potential and how her department could be a good fit for me. I might not have become a psychologist.

Over time, one becomes more directed as strengths become clearer. Midlife now appears more dramatic than ever because we are no longer in an economy when many of us stay with one company for 30 years. In the world of career free agency, our career Turning Points present more frequent crises and opportunities: Either outside circumstances demand a change or internally we experience a push for something different.

OUR CONVERSATION

Dennis, 41, brought extensive notes about work history to our feedback session and used them to describe how his career path had developed to date.

"I graduated from a public high school in Maryland with a very high I.Q. score. I tested 149 as a teenager.

"But I wasn't that interested in classroom-style learning. I was always more of a self-learner. I like to explore and figure out on my own. I tend to work at a fairly quick pace, and classroom instruction a lot of times isn't suited for that.

"I've been working with a therapist for about six months on a variety of things, but one of the things I've learned is that I've got pretty pronounced interpersonal anxiety, which I think came into the school mix.

"So to make a long story short, at the end of high school I didn't know what I wanted to do, but what I did know was that I didn't want any more school. But I don't think I've ever really asked myself what I want to do.

"Early on, it was about finding a line of work I thought was 'respectable,' one that I could earn enough to live on being out on my own. Now I'm in my 40s and I've been in the IT field for 16 or 17 years. I know what I have today isn't what I want, but for the life of me, I can't figure out what I really want to do. That's been a problem for the past two or three years."

It was obvious that Dennis – like many of my clients – was at a key Turning Point in his life. In his case, it was the Midlife Transition, which usually occurs between 38 and 45.

I asked him what he'd enjoyed in high school. "Music, primarily. I was playing instruments in plays and singing, all of that. I did apply to a music school and was rejected, and that was that."

I asked him what types of jobs he'd taken after high school. "I started working as a bank teller. Did that for two or three years and then worked as a customer account representative. I worked for a takeout food place for a year and a half managing delivery and somehow managed to rationalize that as a decision.

"I fell into IT completely by accident, when I had been out of high school for three years."

I asked him what roles in his IT career had come most easily to him and which ones "took more effort and energy from you."

"Well I can tell you that in the whole span of IT, I've only had one job I loved. That was an operational job where I was essentially supporting the computers and the network infrastructure of a company with about 1,200 people at that location. So I was constantly putting out fires. There wasn't a lot of structure in the company, so I essentially got to decide how to do things.

"I liked the pace because it was quick. I didn't have a whole lot of interaction with people. I didn't have direct reports, which I liked because I'm off the chart on the introversion scale."

But Dennis lost that job when his boss was let go and moved to project management with a different company.

"I'm very good at the administrative parts of the position," he said, "planning, communicating, particularly in writing, tactical-level work where the strategy has been set forth for me and I have to go achieve it. I'm better with tactics than strategy.

"I would say I'm good at any part of the job that's analytical, working with data. I love doing that. The parts I'm not really good at are in retrospect the higher-value project management skills. Being able to understand the scope of a project well enough that you can kind of look around the corner and see the train coming before it hits you. Being able to see threats and risks to your project well before they actually happen.

I tend to react to them more than see them in advance.

"Anything involving dealing with people or trying to motivate them is very hard for me due to the combination of introversion and social anxiety. I also tend not to be very visible because I tend to prefer sitting in my cubicle and doing my work. And I think that's a hindrance."

"So you're thinking you want to see about doing something else?" I asked.

"Yes. I know I don't want what I have now. Both my mind and my body are telling me 'You're very unhappy' in different ways."

Dennis was married and had one child, but still had to provide over two-thirds of the family's household income, so he felt there were some economic constraints on what he could do. His wife's job was emotionally rewarding to her but did not pay well.

"Let me add another thing," he said. "Historically I've been able to perform at a good level despite whatever personal things were going on in my life. But the last year and a half has been more and more difficult, and I actually got one of the worst performance reviews this year that I ever got. I actually ranked at the bottom of my team.

"I'm really working to get to the root of it."

I told him he had done a fantastic job at describing the one job he had really loved and that many of the reasons were reflected in his results on the Battery. (Before you go any further, try to guess how Dennis ranks in Classification and Time Frame.)

"You had a lot of very strong abilities," I said, "talents that are kind of happening simultaneously." His Grip score was also high, reflecting natural tenacity.

Dennis ranked as a very strong Specialist, 92nd percentile. "Specialists typically don't feel like everyone else does," I told him. "They don't flow with the group very easily. If they do, they feel out of sorts with themselves. If they say something in a meeting, it's going to sound like it came out of left field."

"I get that a lot," he said.

As he had reported, Dennis also ranked very strongly as an Introvert.

"You're pretty solidly in that world of getting energy from going inside your head," I said, "thinking things through, seeking more structured interactions with individuals or small groups, preferring telephone conversations, e-mail.

"An Introvert/Specialist is what we call the 'professional personality.' This is par excellence the personality of the scientist, the researcher, the person who not only wants to understand the phenomena in depth but also enjoys doing work that's complex without necessarily having to get up and check their ideas with other people doing that research."

Dennis also had a very short Time Frame, perhaps three to six months, which explained his comfort level with the "putting out fires" aspect of the IT job he really loved.

"You're driven for results, you thrive on getting those results," I said.

He scored high in Classification, 80th percentile, which once again went with his ability to rapidly solve problems. "These are the people you bring in as consultants," I added. "Find a problem, tell us what it is. But the opposite side is that managing others can be challenging because someone might come into your office and expect you to listen to their problem, and as they begin to describe it, in your head you're solving it."

"Yeah, I did learn that with my wife. A lot of times she just wants me to listen, but she doesn't want me to solve it, but that took me a few years to figure out." (Of course the question is: Does this age-old marital interaction complaint come down to differing abilities? Classification, however, as we have seen, is not a male characteristic. It is equal opportunity in distribution between the genders.)

"Right," I said. "If you have an ability, you have to use it, and if you don't have an ability, it's easier to see it in others."

"So if you're in an environment like my bank, where it is very regimented and structured, that would appeal more to someone with lower Classification?"

"Yes. You got it."

He also scored very high in Concept Organization, 85th percentile, which I told him could be very helpful in project management. "This is different from Time Frame, which focuses more on the task and the energy involved," I said. "This is about being able to think, 'This is a project that's going to take two years,' and work back from that."

Dennis clearly had a "consultative" problem-solving and decision-making style, and felt he had done well in his one brief experience as IT consultant, which ended when he went "in house."

"I wanted to find out if there was a correlation between the price of energy and how much the company was earning in margin," he said. "Because when prices would spike really high, I wondered if it was due to demand or we were getting gouged.

"So I ran this whole five-year trending analysis that showed they actually make the least when the prices are highest and the most when they're lowest. I probably spent two or three days doing it, and it was fun."

"For you, any kind of problem-solving is when you're working on all cylinders."

"Yes.

But it's not always easy to explain the results to people, for me, anyway."

"Well, if you did a written report, it would be easier."

"Even with those, I sometimes have trouble with people. One time I was asked to do a survey for a golf club. So I did this whole elaborate Web-based survey and collected all the data. I ended up producing a 110-page deliverable.

"And when I did the presentation to the board, the board was, like, 'Hell, what is all this stuff? Who is this guy?'"

"I think that's the Specialist run amok," I told him. "They wanted more of a Generalist approach, more superficial. Your audience is usually about 70 percent Generalists.

"Which means they probably read the executive summary and threw the book away.

"So when you're sitting in a meeting and a problem is coming at you, what's your initial reflexive action? To organize it or to diagnose it and jump to a solution and then work through how you got there?"

Here I was wondering – since both problem-solving abilities are so high – about Dennis' experience when faced with a problem. Having a person focus and become aware of what he does with a problem or an interaction in the here and now is a great way to have him experience his use of abilities.

"To diagnose it, although I would generally say I want to take it away and study it. And I whiteboard stuff a lot."

"Yes. Then you're going to go with the Classification first, that's going to be stronger. Your Concept Organization is going to kick in with the whiteboard, but it's also the Specialist and the introversion. You're not going to just start responding off the top of your head."

Dennis was mid-range in Idea Productivity, which I told him meant that "you're going to have enough ideas. You just don't want to be in a role where you're being asked to come up with all sorts of alternatives, or in a marketing role where you have to overcome people's resistance to your ideas in an off-the-cuff manner."

"I don't like resistance in groups," he said, "because I typically feel like people aren't giving the ideas a chance or they don't understand what I'm talking about."

"Yes. And so engineers typically are low Idea Productivity."

In Spatial Relations, he scored fairly low, however, slightly unusual for someone who was an Introvert and a Specialist. Many of these people are also in the structural world, not the abstract world the way he was. Even though his career was in IT, he had no real facility for building computers. "I'll have fun picking out the one that's best suited to my needs, or looking at specs," he said.

This profile was not unique, I told him, "but it's an interesting twist. But the strong Specialist finding colors everything. It's still about your passion about in-depth or specialized knowledge that drives the whole thing forward."

Among the Specialized Abilities, he was in the 65th percentile or above in the five Learning Channels. His high Design Memory score could be linked closely to creativity and help explain the frustration with his current job. Observation was in the 80th percentile, and when linked with his high Concept Organization gave him an "investigative profile." Verbal Memory was in the 85th percentile, meaning that he could easily absorb information through reading.

Dennis noted that he tended to read very little except for materials related to a hobby or his job except perhaps for a newspaper. I told him this wasn't surprising. "My experience is that the higher people are in Design Memory, the more practical they are in terms of things. And low Idea Productivity also probably pulls for that." His Tonal Memory, learning by listening, was extraordinary – 99th percentile.

"You hear something and you recall it," I said. "You're at a staff meeting and they're talking and you're able to take in information and store it pretty readily. People whose eyes glaze over after five minutes, they're low in Tonal Memory. Their channel kind of got saturated very fast.

"So while you may not look like you're listening to someone who's telling you a problem, you're actually hearing it very well. It's just that you're busy solving it in your head. Listening to something in the car, that's also a way for you to learn something pretty fast."

"Yes. To crystallize my own understanding of an idea, I have to say it out loud. So with the project teams I work with, I'll say, 'Tell me and then stop and let me say it back to you.'"

"And then you let them know that you listened to and understand what they've said."

It turned out he had been using this Learning Channel on the golf course without realizing it. "Because every shot is different, I'll actually have to say out loud all the things that I'm taking into consideration to really have it. Otherwise it's like it's floating around out there, but I haven't really grabbed it. The people I play with kind of think I'm strange, but…"

"Well, it's a Learning Channel that's strong for you. So what."

"Yeah, I'll tell them that," he said, laughing.

His score on Rhythm Memory was in the 95th percentile. This often translates into the ability to learn through movement, another explanation of why he was a good golfer!

"It's also learning through watching another person do a task," I said. "So sitting still for a long period of time during the day has to be deadly for you."

"Which is what I do now."

"Well, you're a restless, energetic guy. This isn't by chance. And now it makes complete sense that school was problematic for you because you're supposed to sit in your chair and pay attention. In school, you have to cover a wide range of things, which doesn't really allow for the Specialist. Sometimes even college doesn't allow for it. Maybe not until you get to graduate school.

"And someone with high Rhythm Memory wants to get up and move around and learn through doing, through a laboratory, through hands-on experiences."

"Right. Give me something to play with and I'll solve it. But don't ask me to sit there and listen." A good feedback consult on results should be a collaborative effort, thinking together to create a story, a new partial narrative.

Of course, Dennis' high Tonal Memory score meant that he could learn by listening. He just would have to be moving around while he listened!

"So Rhythm Memory's high," I told him, "and that's about energy and movement. So you've got high Grip, high Rhythm Memory. You're in perpetual motion. It's nonstop."

His Pitch Discrimination was in the 75th percentile. Not surprisingly, this correlates strongly with music ability, but "it's also more of an aesthetic in the sense that it goes across the senses, so it can come out in decorating and in cooking."

And it turned out that Dennis wrote music, played several instruments and cooked. He had a recording studio in his home.

And golf and music were outlets for abilities he couldn't use at work, at least not in his current job.

Number Memory was also in the 99th percentile, so it was obvious that Dennis could learn quickly in a variety of ways, almost too quickly. People with his profile are highly subject to boredom. "You have a very small learning curve for new things," I told him.

But his low Idea Productivity was helpful in that someone with five Learning Channels and high Idea Productivity would be extremely prone to distraction.

The Ability Battery results contain work types (see Test Drives at the end of the book), work roles that would be "strong matches" or "weak matches" with the individual's talents.

Dennis had carefully read a copy of his report results before coming to our session. He said he had read the section on "weak matches" to his wife, "and she said, 'I don't know if you could pick many jobs in IT that are worse fits for you than the one you are doing.' We were laughing."

I told him, "I think what happens when you're younger is you can override your abilities. But as you get older, the pressure to use what comes easy to us becomes more intense. And that's where people get dissatisfied."

Dennis' Discoveries

The big one for him was the number of Learning Channels – all of them – and the ability to market himself as someone who learns very, very quickly!

Dennis had connected his natural abilities to roles and things he thrived on. The very poor match with his current role was stressful and creating serious problems.

Here was someone with tremendous talents and passion, coupled with powerful problem-solving abilities, who could learn new information fast and teach it to others. Yet his mismatch was creating severe issues for him and his employment.

Dennis, at this Turning Point, has an opportunity to explore work environments that in the near future could allow for greater expression of who he is as well as significantly impact his contribution. Making Dennis into a team leader where he worked through others was not something in the cards but rather fit into some ideal role held by a supervisor for him.

Takeaways

- **For you:** Really focusing on how you dealt successfully with a challenge is a great way to better understand how you use your abilities.
- **For you:** A strong Specialist may have trouble adjusting to a school curriculum until graduate school allows him to function in that role.
- **For coaches:** A good feedback consult on results should be a collaborative effort, thinking together to create a story, a new partial narrative.

MEG'S RESULTS

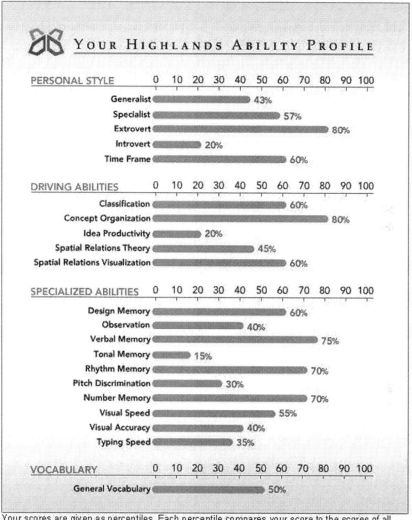

Your scores are given as percentiles. Each percentile compares your score to the scores of all persons who have taken the same worksample.

"On the deaf man's door, you can knock all you want."

— Greek proverb

IX. Meg, 43, Corporate Communications
Seeking the Challenge of Marketing

When we reach midlife, there are all kinds of signals for change ahead. It's a question of heeding the signs. We can keep our head down and stay the course to the detriment of self. Remember it isn't necessarily about making big changes but rather acknowledging what is going on within and without you. You need to incorporate new information about yourself that may have been there all along but only now makes sense.

OUR CONVERSATION

Meg is 43 and works in corporate communications for a cable company. She works primarily in internal communications, mostly with human resources.

I asked her what parts of her job were easy and stressless.

"Probably the meetings with clients are the most stressless," she said.

"And now on the other side," I said, "what are the things you can do but just take you more time, effort and energy?"

"Probably some of the more technical writing I have to do. If I have to communicate the company's corporate goals, there's a lot of industry jargon."

Meg had spent most of her career in financial services and was director of advertising and communications for a financial services organization for 13 years. Earlier she had gone through a management training program at a bank and worked in the marketing department.

In college, she had majored in hotel and restaurant management because she thought she wanted to own a restaurant. She went into banking because the hotel and restaurant market in Philadelphia wasn't very good when she graduated. Right now, she had one child at home and was working part time.

"OK," I said. "When you look ahead five years from now, what are you thinking about, what would your career look like, what would you be doing?"

"I would like to get back into the marketing side of things," she said. "Advertising, marketing. The thing I liked about my role as director of advertising was that I owned a piece of something and I could make decisions and manage a budget and I don't have any of that now."

Meg was a mid-range Specialist, 57th percentile, meaning that this was the world she had to be in first, mastering a skill or knowledge area before moving into a role of influencing or persuading others and working through teams.

"So what is your expertise? What are you the go-to person for?" I asked her.

"I think communication strategy."

She also scored strongly as an Extrovert, somewhat causing a push in another direction for someone heavily involved in writing.

"But I like to share my writing with everybody," she said.

"But you have to write it yourself, right?"

"Hmmm."

"So the Specialist is where you cut yourself off temporarily from other people," I said. "You go into your own head, try to absorb it, get down underneath it and maybe come up with a strategy.

"Usually when you have a Specialist, you have introversion, like the scientists who like to write. Take a writer, even if extreme like J.D. Salinger or Thoreau. Even Cat Stevens/Yusuf Islam goes off into the proverbial woods and cuts himself off from everybody. Specialist/Extrovert is a different category. They're on the one hand pulled to cut themselves off and get into an idea, but they're also pulled to get up and talk to people about it."

This is the push and pull of the mix of Specialist and Extrovert. It is not that it is bizarre, but it is complex and can seem contradictory to others, who more often than not tend to see us as one-dimensional. People want to reduce others to one trait and make them more predictable, but they still want to be fully understood in their own complexity! Honoring complexity in others can help them begin to see your various facets.

Meg was mid-range in Time Frame, meaning that she was most comfortable planning from one to three years out.

I told her the benefit of that was she had some ability to be results-oriented and some ability to do longer range planning, although someone with a high or low score would be more comfortable than she would be at either extreme.

In Classification, she scored in the 60th percentile, high enough that she would clearly need challenge and novelty in the workplace that went beyond using knowledge and experience to solve problems.

"You need novelty, you need the ability to make a decision and move on to the next decision. Think about what you said about needing to own a piece of something. Being a Specialist is about having that turf and being able to own it, and Classification is about having the freedom to make decisions and implement them. Large bureaucratic organizations are probably going to rub you the wrong way."

She agreed, adding she hated situations where a proposal had to get a long series of approvals: "Can't we just make a decision and go?"

"That's the whole collaborative thing," I said. "Low Classification people run large organizations, and for the most part things don't have to be decided immediately and they're going to do it through collaboration."

Meg's highest Driver by far was Concept Organization, not surprising for a writer. "This is logical, methodical, step-by-step thinking," I said. "People who have this high Driver are super-organized in their head. When they write something, it's already written in their head and then they put it on paper. With a low Concept Organization person, the sentences have to be moved around. And writers often have high Concept Organization because they can think of the reader's view."

Meg described her experience: "I loved this work sample (on the Battery). I was moving stuff from the beginning, and, no, this goes here and this goes there, I wished there were more of them. You should see my desk, it's a mess, but I know where everything is, and I have my piles and papers, but that is how I like to work.

"That's how I think through it. OK, these are the main points, and now I got to go to this. And then internally, I think what I am good at is anticipating what the readers' reactions are going to be, knowing your audience. That's what the Concept Organization is, being able to take a student through the steps to get to the answer. It's more of an understanding of the pain points and the sensitivities of a particular topic, like how are employees going to view this.

"So that's more my thinking; well, we can just say here's the way it is. On certain things, there are pain points, especially when you're talking about their bonus or their health insurance coverage."

Taking this ability into the world of strategizing, I said, "Project management is a piece of cake. It's fun for you. 'OK, we have to allocate people, resources, time and energy into the future.' That's almost not work. Low Concept Organization is about having the world organize you. Companies organize us. They tell us when to get there and when to leave."

Meg had a low score in Idea Productivity, which she had no problem with once I explained that the number of ideas had nothing to do with their quality. She had mid-range scores in Spatial Relations Visualization and Spatial Relations Theory.

Her score on Spatial Relations Visualization meant that she had a need for hands-on activity either in the workplace or out of it. In her case, athletic activities such as hiking and biking met that need.

Spatial Relations Theory tends to correlate with ability in interpersonal relations, with diplomats tending to have very high scores (or some people with very high scores gravitating toward diplomacy).

In Meg's case, a mid-range score was sufficient for her to understand both corporate and interpersonal systems.

"That makes sense, yes," she said. "When I was in banking, we wanted to do all these wonderful marketing campaigns, but we needed IT to help us. And, of course, the IT people would say, 'We can't do that and here's why.' And my boss would say, 'I don't want to hear why, we want to do it.'

"So she'd start sending me, and I could understand what they were telling me and we'd figure out a way."

She had mid-range scores in Design Memory and Observation, but scored in the 75th percentile in Verbal Memory, explaining why school had been so easy for her.

Her only low score in the Learning Channels was Tonal Memory. "You have four of the five Learning Channels," I said. "You have a pretty short learning curve in terms of learning new things."

Meg's Discoveries

The important discoveries here are the Specialist/Extrovert scores as well as the Driver, high Concept Organization, all impacted by the Learning Channels working so well. Having high Learning Channels makes it quite easy to market oneself as a quick learner. Her comfort with the financial world makes sense given her mid-range scores in Spatial Relations.

Meg wondered about the wisdom of staying with her current employer because "they're so technical and that's always been a steeper learning curve for me. I'm completely comfortable in the communications world, but as far as deeply understanding our business, it's a steeper learning curve. There's no place for me here beyond where I am today."

She said she liked the flexibility that her company offered for a woman with children at home, but at some point, she would want something more challenging.

What we have is also a combination of her Specialist side with strategy by understanding pain points. While her current role helped her at this point in her career, she longed to "own" more of the business and be her own person. We talked later about a plan to move in that direction two or three years into the future.

Takeaways

- **For you:** People want to reduce others to one trait and make them more predictable, but they still want to be fully understood in their own complexity! Honoring complexity in others helps one see your various facets.
- **For you:** If you are high in Classification, you may need workplace challenges that go beyond using your knowledge and past experience.
- **For coaches:** Being in a role that doesn't fit you exactly can work if you also are developing a plan for the future.

KAREN'S RESULTS

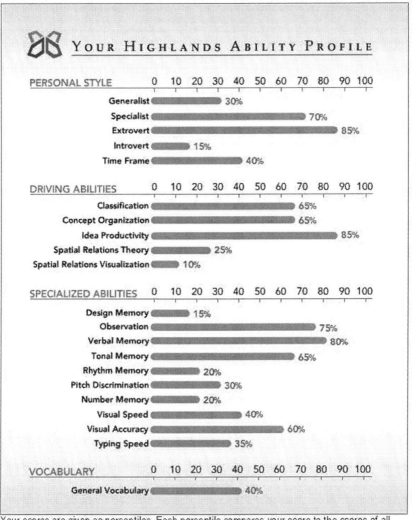

YOUR HIGHLANDS ABILITY PROFILE

PERSONAL STYLE   0 10 20 30 40 50 60 70 80 90 100

Generalist	30%
Specialist	70%
Extrovert	85%
Introvert	15%
Time Frame	40%

DRIVING ABILITIES   0 10 20 30 40 50 60 70 80 90 100

Classification	65%
Concept Organization	65%
Idea Productivity	85%
Spatial Relations Theory	25%
Spatial Relations Visualization	10%

SPECIALIZED ABILITIES   0 10 20 30 40 50 60 70 80 90 100

Design Memory	15%
Observation	75%
Verbal Memory	80%
Tonal Memory	65%
Rhythm Memory	20%
Pitch Discrimination	30%
Number Memory	20%
Visual Speed	40%
Visual Accuracy	60%
Typing Speed	35%

VOCABULARY   0 10 20 30 40 50 60 70 80 90 100

| General Vocabulary | 40% |

Your scores are given as percentiles. Each percentile compares your score to the scores of all persons who have taken the same worksample.

"I believe that one of life's greatest risks is never daring to risk."

— Oprah Winfrey

X. Karen, 45,
Director of Corporate Communications
The Challenge of Multiple Abilities

Frequently, people will glance at their results from the Highlands Ability Battery and get upset when they don't see high percentiles. In their heads, "high" is immediately connected to "good." High SATs, high GMATs, right? Only after the feedback consultation does someone really get the connection between strengths, talents and skills. On the other side of the world are the folks who have many high percentiles who appear to face a whole different set of challenges. Having multiple Driving Abilities can be a challenge to put together into a coherent picture of oneself. Take Karen, a 45-year-old spokeswoman for a midsize engineering company.

OUR CONVERSATION

Karen wrote executive speeches and presentations, handled public relations projects and dealt with the media. She had originally come to the company as a consultant. Her college didn't have a communications major, "so I actually created my own major through general arts and sciences because I wanted to focus on graphic design as well. My major was really English, journalism and graphic design together. After college, I freelanced and worked for different newspapers. I did some TV work."

She got married, had a baby and switched to corporate communications with a large company, where she spent 13 years. She then decided she needed a break. She did some consulting and then moved to a communications director position with another company. But within a year, the company's stock dropped dramatically and her entire department was eliminated.

Karen was typical of many of the clients I deal with. The days of spending your entire career with one company are pretty much over, and people talk more and more about "portable skills." But that doesn't answer the question of what skills and talents really enable an individual to navigate in the new economy. The Ability Battery could answer only the question of what her hardwired abilities are and, therefore, the type of work she could do easily and do well.

This is what Karen and I had to find out together.

"So tell me," I said, "looking at your career, what role would you say that you were in that gave you the most satisfaction? Where were you using your talents the most?"

"I would say when I had my own business when it was going well."

"What was it about it?" I asked.

"The freedom, being able to do anything and not just put in a certain little box. Within a corporation, you're told, 'This is your area and this is what you do despite what other skills you have.'

"As a consultant, once you're hired for a certain thing and your value is seen for that, sometimes you can broaden how a client sees your work.

"So when you think about it, what came easily to you in all these different roles?"

"Developing ideas, conceptualizing and organizing," she said. "Writing, although sometimes it's more difficult the more I really care about something. It's kind of a Catch-22."

"So what have you done that takes more time, effort and energy?" I asked her.

"Things that are routine. I sometimes have difficulty doing something the same way twice. And anything with numbers, things with really technical language, things that are mechanically oriented."

I asked her what role she saw for herself in five years.

"Something where I can use more creativity," she said. "Perhaps in a management role, but I'm not sure. There are things in management that I haven't really liked."

Karen scored in the 70th percentile as a Specialist and also an Extrovert, the "Performing Personality."

"This is the person who has an area of expertise and then they enjoy getting up and telling people about it," I said, "performing in front of others, connecting with people about it. It's going on talk shows and having an expertise and expanding and enjoying that role."

"I almost had a talk show. That's funny," she said.

I told her, "When I've seen leaders who are Extroverted Specialists, it's about people who are very passionate about an area and then they're able to get and gather people around them who can get excited about the vision that the leader is expressing. That environment is pretty important for the Extroverted Specialist because of that give and take, the exchange."

Karen scored mid-range in Time Frame. "The benefit of that," I told her, "is often that this is not going to be what you're known for. You can be results-oriented or you can think strategically, depending on your needs and the needs of people around you."

She also scored in the 65th percentile in Classification, with its mix of rapid problem-solving and decision-making capability and tendency toward impatience or even arrogance. Karen liked painting as a hobby, and I mentioned that "art critics are high in Classification."

"Art critics?" she asked.

"Yes. They find flaws. Artists themselves are 'helped' if they are lower in Classification because if you have high Classification as an artist, it's hard to get things done. They get disgruntled with what they're doing because they see a flaw in it and they just can't complete it, so they're very critical of their own work."

"So this doesn't mean that if you're high Classification, you can't handle crises?" she wondered.

"No, it means just the opposite. That if your job was routine, that would be stressful after a while."

I told her about a career experience, the first real job I had just after getting my doctorate. I was executive director for the Society for the Prevention of Cruelty to Children, and I had to constantly be making quick decisions on whether to remove children from their homes. I'm low in Classification, and as I got into the work, I realized that this job would be relentless and nonstop decision-making stress if I continued and wanted to do well. I needed to add skills.

After taking various courses to build my skills in decision-making, I was able to manage the stress better. But it wasn't until I built the agency enough so I could hire someone who enjoyed that kind of fast-paced diagnostic problem-solving, decision-making that I could relax and focus on what I did well – which was generate program ideas, build programs and select and hire great people.

Fast-forward 15 years. Upon taking the Battery, I came to see with some reflection that my "choices" or areas I saw as talents were "dictated" by my own ability set (low Classification and low Concept Organization, high Generalist and high Idea Productivity).

It completely blew my mind!

Karen mentioned that in her newspaper work, she was, of course, constantly faced with deadlines. "Sometimes you had multiple stories to file, and I enjoyed going out and covering stories, talking to people, coming up with ways to say it, but the deadline part did get very stressful." In that area, I told her it would actually have been more helpful to have had a low Time Frame, so she could have thought more in terms of the immediate story.

It brought to mind another journalist client of mine who never liked to work on stories that took weeks or months. He liked the fast turnover, seeing his articles in print regularly.

Karen was also in the 65th percentile in Concept Organization, which I told her could almost be termed "the writer's ability" to construct a story step-by-step. "People who have this high are very organized in their head, very systematic," I said. "They may not be organized in their outside world in terms of their desk or whatever, but internally things are very tight. So when people with high

Concept Organization write something, it usually doesn't need a lot of editing."

Karen wasn't sure this matched up with her experience. She recalled an extremely demanding editor who insisted that she do an outline for every story and plug facts in. "She was so mean and brutal," Karen said. "I thought I had A.D.D. So I'm just wondering whether some of this can be a learned thing, or it's pretty intrinsic."

"I'd look at this a little differently," I said. "Just because you have an ability doesn't mean you know how to use it. That editor gave you some skills that built onto an already existing ability. And, for instance, if someone doesn't take courses in project management, they may not be able to do that just because they can think logically."

And looking at it from the opposite direction, I told her, people low in Classification can become rapid problem-solvers in areas where they have accumulated considerable experience: They have a virtual database in their heads.

Also, people with low Concept Organization can be very organized. They just have to work harder at it. My guess was that her editor was a low Concept Organization person who thought everyone should approach the task the same as herself...but there is more to this as we look at Karen's Idea Productivity.

Her Idea Productivity score was extremely high, in the 85th percentile. "It's like having a perpetual brainstorm in your head," I said. "All the popcorn is popping simultaneously. In terms of influence and persuasion, this makes a big difference. It's about "When a boss says, 'This is what I want you to do,' that's the worst thing to tell someone with high Idea Productivity because you don't have to have them on board at that moment."

"Wow. This is so me, this part."

I added that having high Concept Organization would to some extent mitigate her high Idea Productivity, so she would be likely to filter out bad ideas rather than simply pass them on.

I asked Karen if there was any opportunity for brainstorming at her company. She said this rarely happened and gave me an account of one such session that she found extremely frustrating. "No one ever does that here," she said, "and when they finally did it, it was so punishing. I was the only one coming up with ideas, and as soon as I did, people would find all the things wrong with them."

"Exactly," I said. "They didn't know the rules." She had experienced the frustration of someone having an ability and being unable to use it productively.

Karen scored low in both areas of Spatial Relations, placing her clearly in the abstract world of teachers, painters and CEOs rather than the structural world of scientists and engineers.

I told her, "It would be very hard for you to do your job currently if you were in the structural world because most of the people who are asking you questions are in the abstract world and you're dealing with an abstraction called a corporation, which is an agreed-on series of relationships that are really not very hands-on kinds of things."

Karen was low in Design Memory but high in Observation, 75th percentile, reflecting such abilities as reading body language or noticing small changes in the environment, another classic writer's skill.

"Someone is asking you a question and you're able to pick up the real question the person is asking. Reading between the lines is very simple for you. You walk into a restaurant and you notice all kinds of people and colors."

Karen also scored high on Verbal Memory, 80th percentile, but was somewhat baffled when she remembered her difficulty learning lines for school plays. I told her this was fairly common for people with such high Idea Productivity: "There are too many competing ideas."

KAREN'S DISCOVERIES

Here Karen realizes that her three Drivers are parts of her that she uses all the time and account for the speed with which she processes information and then expresses it to others. She clearly connected her

Personal Work Style (Extrovert/Specialist) and her ability to persuade and influence while creating on her feet!

Karen is on an interesting journey in a role that allows her to express parts of herself while leaving other parts relatively underused.

Problems are compounded by the fact that she cares about the company and feels valued. What does she do?

The first step is always to take several months to incorporate the information from the Battery feedback. The second step is to articulate the information in a way that others understand. We call that part "self-marketing." The goal is to send consistent messages about your hardwiring so that others come to define you in the way you are doing.

In a future book, we will explore the other factors and how people put together plans based on the seven other factors.

Takeaways

- **For coaches:** Having an ability doesn't mean knowing how to use it. Skills are what turn our abilities into talents.
- **For you:** People low in Classification become rapid problem-solvers in areas where they have accumulated considerable experience.
- **For you:** The Battery is an objective way of developing your own narrative.

HEATHER'S RESULTS

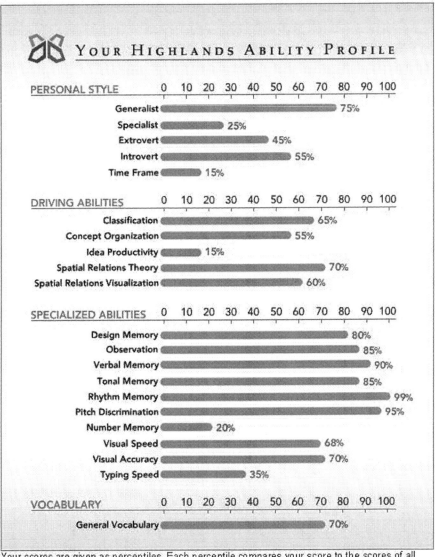

YOUR HIGHLANDS ABILITY PROFILE

PERSONAL STYLE   0 10 20 30 40 50 60 70 80 90 100

- Generalist — 75%
- Specialist — 25%
- Extrovert — 45%
- Introvert — 55%
- Time Frame — 15%

DRIVING ABILITIES   0 10 20 30 40 50 60 70 80 90 100

- Classification — 65%
- Concept Organization — 55%
- Idea Productivity — 15%
- Spatial Relations Theory — 70%
- Spatial Relations Visualization — 60%

SPECIALIZED ABILITIES   0 10 20 30 40 50 60 70 80 90 100

- Design Memory — 80%
- Observation — 85%
- Verbal Memory — 90%
- Tonal Memory — 85%
- Rhythm Memory — 99%
- Pitch Discrimination — 95%
- Number Memory — 20%
- Visual Speed — 68%
- Visual Accuracy — 70%
- Typing Speed — 35%

VOCABULARY   0 10 20 30 40 50 60 70 80 90 100

- General Vocabulary — 70%

Your scores are given as percentiles. Each percentile compares your score to the scores of all persons who have taken the same worksample.

"A good hockey player plays where the puck is. A great hockey player plays where it's going to be."

– Wayne Gretzky

XI. Heather, 46, Trainer of IT Managers
Wondering if it's Time to Leave

When one is hardwired to be in the world of things and concrete objects, it is challenging to find satisfaction in the world of ambiguities, ideas and relationships – or what we call the abstract world. In the world of downsizing, layoffs and mergers, however, people may be flung into ill-fitting work roles. In the midst of a phase in which one thinks she is building a career and has adopted a work role and building skills, along comes an uncalled-for change from the external world. Our resilience is challenged.

This doesn't mean that we aren't responsible for ourselves. In fact, having a clear understanding of our abilities as well as a career vision allows us to communicate clearly how each of us contributes.

OUR CONVERSATION

Heather is 46. She worked for a large brokerage firm, and her title was "project portfolio manager," which she said meant essentially that she was an analyst involved in training IT project managers.

Heather was an accounting major and computer science minor in college. "I had a tough time deciding what I wanted to do. Numbers and I get along pretty well, so it was a good fit there. The computer stuff was new and up-and-coming."

She had always worked in corporations rather than public accounting, starting with a clothing manufacturer, then moving to a chemical treatment company and finally to Lockheed Martin. "So I've done a lot of moving.

"It was at Lockheed Martin that I made the shift from accounting to project management. She said. "Their financial systems and processes needed to be streamlined and made more efficient, and when you start that it's amazing how you get selected to keep doing it."

"Did you enjoy it?" I asked.

"Loved it. I knew I was making an impact on what we did. I was making things profitable and people had an easier time doing their job and I could help them and help train them in new activities. It was just a challenge that I liked."

She was also traveling around the U.S. for the company and enjoyed that for a while but eventually became bored and left. "It became maintenance," she said. "I was doing the same thing every day."

In her latest job, however, Heather found herself frustrated by the corporation's resistance to change.

"They don't really appreciate having anybody else give them ideas," she said. "We think we're very open-minded, but we're not. You hate to say that about your company, but it's true.

"We do a lot of great things, we're very broad-thinking about markets, but each area selects its own stuff and you might as well be an auditor coming in. They didn't want to hear it, so I ended up moving into the project management office.

"It's an interesting thing now to be able to train people, which I guess I like to do most of the time. There are always one or two exceptions, but it's pretty rewarding. You see them frustrated at first and all of a sudden the light starts turning on, and wow, they get excited about wanting to learn more and that's the best part."

Heather said the department was eventually decentralized, though, and "we had no cohesion anymore. I go on vacation and I beg, borrow and steal to get someone to cover for me for a week."

"OK, so looking ahead five years from now, what do you want to be doing?" I asked her.

"Well, if I want to shift in any way to a new kind of thing, I want to do that in the next five years. I don't want to be 60 and going, 'Well, let's try something new.'

"Part of me thinks about leaving the company and other parts of me say there are other areas here I want to explore and the company itself is really great. I really like the people. I like the atmosphere."

I asked her to think harder about what she would most like to do, regardless of whether it meant leaving the company.

"I always had a lot of interest in computer stuff in Web development, but if I wanted to do that, I wouldn't do it here. We're not advanced enough. I'd want to be in the leading-edge technology. They outsource for that."

On the Ability Battery, Heather scored as a Generalist, 75th percentile. (Could you tell from her frequent use of "we"?)

"Generalists make up 70 percent of the population," I told her, "and they see the world from a common perspective. They share a common framework for understanding and viewing things, and this makes it easier for them to communicate because they have that shared reference.

"These are the folks who approach the world of work from the idea of working with and through others to achieve an organization's ends. They are team players without even thinking about it. They can occupy a variety of roles on the team depending on what's needed.

"They can be facilitators or leaders, it doesn't make a difference, but they do depend on having an environment that's stimulating, where they can move through things pretty rapidly, keep lots of balls in the air. It's about having a wide range of interests but not being an expert in any area. Feeling like, 'OK, I got enough of this now. I know it now and get me to another area.' It's a mile-wide-and-inch-deep approach to knowledge.

"Generalists tend to wind up in management roles. They find it easy to delegate. Specialists have a harder time delegating. They want to own the end result much more. Does that make sense to you?"

"It's funny," she said. "I think I started out life a little bit more as a Specialist, and as I'm getting older, I'm becoming more of a Generalist."

"Hold off on that," I said. "The theory is that over time, instead of becoming something else we become more of who we are. For you, another way to think about what you just said is that maybe you were always a Generalist, but you performed Specialist activities and that wasn't sufficient. Just being an accountant wasn't sufficient."

"Not for me," she said.

Heather scored almost in the middle on the Introvert/Extrovert scale, meaning that she needed to shift between the two.

"Generalists have this peculiar team-oriented perspective," I told her, "but they also tend to keep their distance and be more neutral. It's a push-pull combination. The extroverted part helps you in persuading and influencing. You look for a stimulating emotional environment where people are excited. Any other environment is going to take energy from you."

She also had a short Time Frame, which made it easy for her to function in a very results-oriented environment. But in terms of the career work she and I were doing, it made it tougher to plan ahead.

Heather was in the 65th percentile in Classification, high enough for her to solve problems quickly and easily but not so high as to make her super-critical in dealing with others or herself.

Her Concept Organization score was high enough, 55th percentile, for her to basically have a "consultative decision-making" style.

"That's the person brought in as a consultant to identify a problem and help people draw the steps they need to solve the problem," I explained.

She scored low on Idea Productivity, which I told her "is really about focusing on roles where quality ideas count. It's about focus and follow-through, making things happen rather than thinking outside the box."

In Spatial Relations Theory, she scored in the 70th percentile, but in Spatial Relations Visualization, she was mid-range.

Her score combination was difficult to interpret — mid-range scores on the Spatial Relations Visualization work sample often are — so for further guidance I asked her about hobbies and interests outside work. She had earlier said she enjoyed both playing and listening to classical music. She also did plumbing, woodworking and home repairs. "It's kind of weird," she said.

"The guy neighbors come and borrow my tools. It's kind of embarrassing."

"Too bad you don't live next door to me," I said. "But your results make a little more sense to me now. You have Spatial Relations Theory, which is about the theoretical workings of the mechanical universe. You have this ability to understand how systems work, mechanical systems as well as interpersonal systems.

"You might not know how the theory of relativity works, but if you paid attention and thought about it and read about it, you'd understand it.

"In Spatial Relations Visualization, the mid-range score is tough to understand. If you were in the 70th percentile, you'd have to be in the tangible world of making and doing things with your hands. It seems you're halfway in that world so you need this plumbing and woodworking and playing the piano. You're compelled to do this stuff because your job may be more in the abstract world."

"Well, I guess that's my one gripe here," she said. "We don't have a product the way we had at Boeing. You can see the results of electricity, but you can't see electricity. I can see planes. I can see chemicals."

Among the Learning Channels, she scored in the 80th percentile in Design Memory. "If you have a manual with pictures in it, a trend analysis, a chart – that sticks in your head."

"It's funny," she said, "whenever I can, I tend to present in pictures."

"Well, if you're surrounded by engineers, it makes complete sense because generally as a group they are likely to be low Tonal Memory and therefore they can't listen very long," I said.

She also scored high in Observation, 85th percentile. "It's about being in highly stimulating environments and being able to pick up and notice all kinds of things," I said. "It could also come out in being observant of small details in woodworking."

She also scored very high in Verbal Memory and in the so-called Musical Abilities – Tonal Memory, Rhythm Memory and Pitch Discrimination.

HEATHER'S DISCOVERIES

Heather was surprised and delighted by my description of her. "You're a fast learner with multiple ways of taking in new information," I told her. "You thrive on new problems and novel situations. You can construct and design things and see and deal with higher-level concepts pretty easily. It's a little unusual, an experience of push-pull, to find someone with a team orientation who's this hands-on in the tangible world."

As I handed her a copy of my book Don't Waste Your Talent, I suggested she take an especially close look at the Family of Origin section and ask herself: "What did your family teach you about the world of work? What did they tell you before you had your own intelligence and separate identity to think for yourself? What did they communicate nonverbally about the world of work? Also consider Values: What did your family teach about values? What are the values that have emerged that pull you into the future?" (Note that there is a Family of Origin exercise in the Test Drives section at the end of this book.)

Heather had plenty of information to ponder over the next few days and weeks as she developed a Personal Vision, including experiences that started well before her work life as well as preparing her self-marketing 90-second elevator speech for her future role within her company!

Takeaways

- **For teams:** Generalists can play pretty much any role depending on what's needed as long as they are in a stimulating environment
- **For you:** The "Ambivert" position does prove flexibility as long as one is conscious about one's own needs.
- **For coaches:** Mid-range scores in Spatial Relations can be difficult to interpret. Try to find out about the client's hobbies and other interests outside work.

Detour - Family of Origin Influence

(June, 36, Organizational Development)

"It was pretty interesting to do the Career Time Line (see Test Drives for your opportunity to try this) Line exercise. I realized that I had left off a couple of jobs – there were several times when I had a job that I didn't really like during the day and a part-time job at night that I really did like. Even now, I've got my own business (skimpy though it may be), I volunteer for Business Volunteers for the Arts, and I do a ton of stuff with my church. And this "job" is definitely a smiley face for me. It tells me that I enjoy having a combination of jobs.

"I thought a lot about my family's influence. There was so much pressure to keep working – or rather to stay single and have a career. I also was really tied into the money; it was definitely a security issue. Although now, I have to laugh because we are existing on so little now it's crazy. Who would have thought?!! Not that I wouldn't mind having more, just not at a "cost" of boredom."

* * *

Jackie's Results

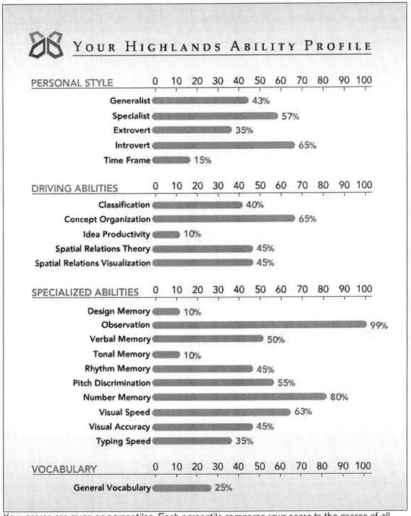

Your scores are given as percentiles. Each percentile compares your score to the scores of all persons who have taken the same worksample.

"If you don't know where you are going, you will wind up somewhere else."

– Yogi Berra

XII. Jackie, 46, Senior HR Administrator
Finding What's Best for You in the Company

A theme emerges, especially when folks in their 40s come in to discuss their Battery results. Often there is a realization that where they ended up – while it may in fact be a fine place – was the result of "just circumstances," luck or happenstance. In some cases, that is presented as not good enough or will be judged as inadequate.

In contrast is the more important question of taking responsibility more fully now for one's career, adding a navigational component. It is in the second half of life that you can begin to shape what lies ahead.

At the same time, one often finds a paralysis, a low-level fear of change and comfort with the status quo. From the organizational perspective, is being contented and doing the job acceptable? Or is the task of the organization to provide opportunities for employees to grow their talents? It does come down to the organizational culture and what is really valued vs. what is given lip service.

OUR CONVERSATION

Jackie is 46, the senior human resources administrator for a large national company. She administers programs, including relocation, tuition reimbursement, and the tracking of contractors and consultants.

"My day-to-day duties are mostly independent, with a lot of computer work, tracking, spreadsheets, processing requests on the Internet," she said.

I asked how she got to her present job, and she said it was "kind of just circumstance." Although it is phrased in different ways, it's something that many of my clients say. We more often than not are lucky, e.g., my meeting the psychology professor. However, at some point, one becomes responsible for one's direction. Then it is also about preparing and putting oneself in circumstances for the opportunity that moves you in the direction where you can further articulate who you are and what your contribution will be.

"I was doing a co-op in high school for a company that made pipe fittings," she said. "I started in the accounting department as a file clerk. They needed a data entry clerk, and they started training me for that.

"My Dad wanted me to go to college because I was the oldest and I was the first in the family to get a high school diploma. But they offered me a full-time job at $5 an hour, which was a lot back then. So I took it, got married and started a family."

Jackie worked in data entry for about 13 years for three companies, got laid off and wound up working in the shipping and receiving department of a company that made racing cars. "I actually created an inventory system for them," she said. "I stayed there eight or nine years. I loved that job. It was very physical. It was pretty independent work.

"I love cars. My father was a mechanic, and we lived next door to his business, so I was always around cars."

But the job didn't pay enough, and she eventually wound up in data entry for another company and then bid on and got a secretarial position in the company's HR department.

"I really liked that," she said. "I've never had a job I didn't like." She spent 11 years there before going to her current company two years before our meeting.

I asked her what she wanted to be doing in five years.

"I'm pretty convinced I'd still like to be working in the HR area," she said. "I did start working this year on a business degree, and maybe I'd transfer into organizational development. But I'm pretty sure I don't want to be in any kind of management."

On the Ability Battery, Jackie was a mid-range Specialist, 57th percentile. I explained to her how this often plays out in the corporate world, with someone developing an expertise and later sharing it as a Generalist.

"Let's say you're the go-to person for anything that someone needs to know about benefits," I said. "More and more you start to participate in committees and teams. That becomes easier because a Generalist has a natural feel for how teams work, as long as you have that expertise behind you. Without it, your confidence will go down the tubes.

"It's easier for you to influence and work with a team towards goals than someone who's purely a Specialist because they have to be seen as an expert at all times. Someone who is more of a blend, like yourself, doesn't always have to be seen as an expert."

Jackie wasn't surprised at this finding. But what did surprise her was that she scored in the 65th percentile as an Introvert.

"I believe that people become more who they're meant to be as time goes on," I said. "We appear to shed the influence of our Family of Origin, and pleasing other people. So someone who was supposed to be an Introvert had to be an Extrovert to survive and now they can revert to what they wanted to be all along."

Carl Jung believed that we each possess introversion and extroversion as part of who we are. He thought that we spend the first part of our lives developing our Extrovert side and then, after the midlife crisis, we spend the next period bringing ourselves into balance and develop our introverted side.

Jackie had said that on some of the questions in that section of the Battery: "It just depends on the day I'm answering."

I suggested that she might be more an "Ambivert," someone with an emotional foot in both worlds. "So someone who's an Ambivert with a pull towards the Introvert side can be in the extroverted world for a period of time," I said. "They just can't stay there all the time. They can't go from meeting to meeting to meeting without time to recoup and energize by going inside for a while. There are times in the feedback consultation/conversation especially when we are talking about the E-I dimension that we need to adjust.

"On the other hand, someone who has a slight preference for introversion is going to eventually be tired of being in the woods by themselves and seek out contact with other people."

We talked about how this played out in non-work situations. At parties, how introverted or extroverted she was depended on whether she knew other people there and whether she was in her comfort zone. If she stepped into a hotel elevator and didn't know anyone, she would usually say something to someone "unless it's someone in there that's giving off a vibe that makes me uncomfortable.

"When I was younger, I was most definitely an Introvert. Having children and getting a divorce, I can see where I became more of an Extrovert as a means of survival.

I don't often think, 'God I really want to go out and be around people,' but I can be around people and thinking, 'God, I can't wait to get home and be alone.'"

Jackie scored low in Time Frame, which she immediately related to her difficulty planning for higher education. Instead, I offered a positive perspective. I told her, "This is a results-oriented base. It's about being in an environment where you can turn things around and move on to the next project." I wanted Jackie to see that, yes, it was related to planning and higher education completion at a personal level, but that her success was also reflected in this result.

She scored mid-range in Classification, and I asked her, "What do you feel like when you have a new problem that comes across your desk that you haven't solved before?"

"Some anxiety," she said. "Intimidation sometimes, but I really want to get the answer."

"Let's say you're having several new ones every day," I said.

"I can't fix everything."

"So that's the difference," I said. "The person who's high in Classification wants that all the time. They don't want the routine. They don't want to solve a problem they've solved before. I do think yours is high enough that you need a certain level of novelty, even though it might cause anxiety, to be able to kind of keep your edge.

But the lower score is also good because it makes it easier for you to listen and be relatively patient with other people."

"I've had that at work, I don't have that at home," she said. "I just think people at home should be able to get it quicker because they're used to me."

Her Concept Organization was higher, 65th percentile, which surprised her. But when she realized that her e-mails needed little editing and she really didn't need to consult her schedule, she got a sense of this.

"Analytic thinking is enjoying things that are step-by-step. When you communicate to other people, do you think they follow you when you talk?"

"It depends. I think I'm a much better written communicator than verbal."

"That's the introversion coming out," I said. "If you're more introverted and high in Concept Organization, you're going to want to be able to think through what you're going to say before you say it, and once you think it through, it's going to come out organized. Extroverts say whatever is on the top of their head."

I suggested that she consider training functions within HR because people with high Concept Organization are often good teachers. "They have to be able to take the student and say, 'OK, here are the steps.'"

She said she would have to do this in written rather than oral form, and I told her, "Think about creating training manuals then. That's where you get to write, and it's more introverted."

Jackie scored low in Idea Productivity, and like many people who do so, she thought that was a negative. As usual, I reassured her that this had nothing to do with the quality of ideas but was an operating style, not a sign of intelligence or lack of it.

"Low Idea Productivity people are more concerned with focus and follow-through," I said. "Most people who lead organizations are low Idea Productivity. This doesn't mean you should lead this company. I'm not saying that.

"You're going to be able to put the slides together for a PowerPoint presentation pretty easily in a logical order while someone with low Concept Organization might have lots more ideas but may not be able to figure what's a good way to present them."

"So that person and I might be able to work together," she said.

"Yes. That's the whole idea of the team thing."

She was mid-range in Spatial Relations, which usually indicates roughly equal comfort in the abstract and concrete worlds. She did add that "mechanical things come much easier to me than theory."

I asked her what hobbies and interests she had outside work, and she said she liked to play volleyball, cook, clean and do home repairs.

If her score had been high rather than mid-range, I said, she almost surely would have needed to find outlets for this hands-on ability in the workplace.

She had a very low score in Design Memory but a very high one, 99th percentile, in Observation. "Working in a very visually stimulating environment is going to very distracting," I said. "For you to do your work, you'd have to close yourself off."

"So cubicles are a good thing for me."

"Yes, if you can get rid of the sound, people walking by."

Jackie's Tonal Memory score was low, so she clearly would have trouble remembering what she'd heard, although her low Classification score probably made her a good listener. "You'll remember generalities, not specifics," I said. "You can tape-record lectures, you can take notes."

She had a fairly high score in Pitch Discrimination, 55th percentile, and I told her this expresses itself across the senses, not just in hearing. "It could be the seasoning in a meal," I said.

"Typically things aren't seasoned enough for me," she said. She was high in Number Memory, but did not see herself in a field like accounting.

"That wouldn't be a challenge," she said. "That would be boring."

"Well, the natural ability is there," I said. "You have to recognize that you have the talent." However having a natural ability or even a talent doesn't mean that it coincides with our interests or even with the other abilities!

JACKIE'S DISCOVERIES

Jackie was taken aback by the identification of her strengths: her natural hardwiring, her high Concept Organization coupled with her introversion as well as being driven for results (low Time Frame). Additionally, Jackie "got" the concept of how teams are strengthened by members who possess differing abilities.

When I look at this consult, I feel it wasn't a great one. I don't think I touched this person. I didn't get past her reluctance to engage her passion – her Specialist side. One can see moments during the consult when she was engaged and excited when working in more tangible worlds and less with strictly abstract, people-oriented activities. My sense is that her mid-range scores in the Spatial Relations would need to be explored in the future. I am relieved to say that in our follow-up workshop, we were able to further explore them!

Takeaways

- **For you:** People with high Concept Organization can excel in teaching roles because they can take a student through the various steps of solving a problem or reaching a conclusion.
- **For teams:** A member with high Idea Productivity and one with high Concept Organization can be a very good pairing.

JOHN'S RESULTS

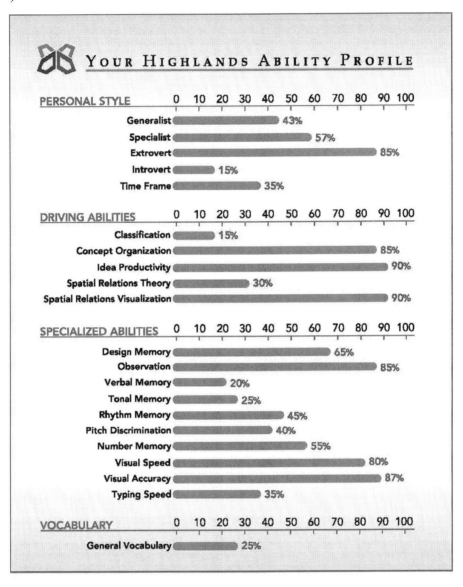

YOUR HIGHLANDS ABILITY PROFILE

PERSONAL STYLE 0 10 20 30 40 50 60 70 80 90 100

- Generalist — 43%
- Specialist — 57%
- Extrovert — 85%
- Introvert — 15%
- Time Frame — 35%

DRIVING ABILITIES 0 10 20 30 40 50 60 70 80 90 100

- Classification — 15%
- Concept Organization — 85%
- Idea Productivity — 90%
- Spatial Relations Theory — 30%
- Spatial Relations Visualization — 90%

SPECIALIZED ABILITIES 0 10 20 30 40 50 60 70 80 90 100

- Design Memory — 65%
- Observation — 85%
- Verbal Memory — 20%
- Tonal Memory — 25%
- Rhythm Memory — 45%
- Pitch Discrimination — 40%
- Number Memory — 55%
- Visual Speed — 80%
- Visual Accuracy — 87%
- Typing Speed — 35%

VOCABULARY 0 10 20 30 40 50 60 70 80 90 100

- General Vocabulary — 25%

"If we are facing in the right direction, all we have to do is keep on walking."

— Buddhist proverb

XIII. John, 47, Senior Analyst in Engineering
Sherlock Holmes and the "Investigative" Profile

Turning points in our lives can be stimulated by unforeseen circumstances. Outsourcing is one common event. However things get considerably more complex when an event like outsourcing occurs as we are already approaching a time to think anew our careers.

John was a 47-year-old senior analyst in Informational technology with a large insurance company.

OUR CONVERSATION

"I take requirements and gather requirements and turn those into a living, breathing IT system," he said.

He had attended a training center for computer programming right out of high school and gone to work for a major pharmaceutical company. He found the work easy, and "I would actually get to talk to people that were doing the work in the pharmaceutical company, the financial people and so forth, and figure out the best way to solve a problem, or get the information they were looking for."

This was followed by a series of corporate and consulting jobs in customer support, programming and sales. He said he particularly enjoyed "people-oriented work. At some point in time, you get sick of just doing the research and writing code."

John said he took the Ability Battery because a co-worker had found it useful rather than due to any particular career development. But it turned out that his job was likely to be outsourced. And he was looking for a new role in the company that would allow him to stay.

"So actually this workshop (John was also attending a corporate-sponsored workshop that we had developed for the company) may be happening for you at a good time then," I said.

"That's what I'm thinking, too."

I encouraged him to "look at the Ability Battery in terms of how easy or stress-free you might find some of the new pieces of this role that you'd like to stay with. You're a relatively young person. You've got at least one more career in you."

I asked him what role he saw for himself in five years.

"A services role because that's where the world is going," he said. "I would like to gain those skills to work with vendors and negotiate and lead, but remain technical because that's what got me where I'm at and I can't just ignore that.

"So in the best of both worlds, I'd be doing pretty much what I'm doing now, which is being very technical and yet being able to communicate with end users and management on projects and run projects and maintain them. That's ideally what I'd still be doing.

"I don't want to be vice president, I really don't. I don't have the skills or real desire to do that, but I would like to be useful and I like to make a difference, and to be honest, I don't have another trade I can go to unless I buy a 7-11 or something like that. I'm ready to lead people. I've had the experience."

John was a mid-range Specialist, so I encouraged him to think of himself as a Specialist first and a Generalist second.

"That mid-range 30-year-old having all those direct reports was just a little bit early, perhaps," I told him. "Unless the Specialist has expertise, it's really hard to feel confident and competent. Then it's moving into the Generalist world, having and maintaining an area of expertise."

"That's me, yes."

The Battery also indicated that John was an Extrovert, and I explained the idea of the Extrovert/Specialist as in some ways a performer. "It seems there's an ease with people you have," I told him.

"In your case, it seems like the Specialist and Extrovert is there in terms of performing and expertise that could mean talking about selling people, selling them on a perspective, selling them on a vision of moving forward and then also being able to be this team-oriented person.

"That's when you combine the Extrovert and the Generalist into this world of influencing and persuading others in terms of a direction, in terms of how they think about things, moving forward. Buy it?"

"Yes."

"Have I wowed you? Talk to me."

"I think you're kind of wowing me in that you've got me pegged, you know. I really do like the Specialist area. It's satisfying to be seen as the go-to guy. Yet that's not all there is in the world."

I told John that while most leaders are primarily Generalists, "in the IT industry, communications, the cable industry and pharmaceuticals, there are leaders who are Extroverted Specialists."

John's Time Frame score was slightly on the low side, 35th percentile. "That would say to me that you're comfortable thinking a year ahead," I said.

He told me that he had enjoyed working on some long-term projects but that there had been intermediate steps, and "I think without those steps it would have been frustrating."

"You're a person who's results-oriented," I said. "Would you agree with that?"

"I would, yes."

We then discussed the Driving Abilities, reminding John that "satisfaction comes from using your abilities and dissatisfaction comes from not being able to use your abilities."

He had a low Classification score, and I explained how this lent itself to a more deliberate, reflective decision-making problem-solving style when faced with new problems, and avoiding situations in which he had to deal with a series of new problems quickly.

John said he actually had done fairly well in some situations like that, although he found it stressful. I attributed this mostly to his having expertise in those areas and drawing on that. "Just because you're low in Classification doesn't mean you can't be for a limited period of time in a fast-paced, ambiguous decision-making role."

In Concept Organization, John had a very high score – 85th percentile. Not surprisingly, he had found this part of the test easier than the Classification section.

"This is the engineers' or research scientists' ability par excellence," I said. "They don't need lots of organization tools around them. Their office space may not be particularly well organized, but inside their head, they're specially organized. People high in this ability are often in roles like project management, writing software. Writers often times are high in Concept Organization, people who edit the work of others for a living.

"Now, how do you see this one in your life?"

"You know, I think it hits me. I can usually take information from a bunch of different sources and put it together or sum it up in a way that's logical to me. In my head, I know what needs to be done, and it just kind of flows out."

The Ability Battery is a complex instrument. "Not all abilities flow in the same direction," I told John. And his high score in Idea Productivity proved that.

"Here you went to town," I said. "You just wrote and wrote and wrote. And that's really what we were measuring – how many ideas. Whether they were good or bad, we didn't care, just how many ideas you had in this short period of time.

"Having high Idea Productivity is useful in roles where you have to convince and persuade other people because you can come up with lots of different ways to overcome resistance," I said, "to have them consider alternatives and to sell an idea or a concept. Tell me your thoughts about this."

"It's fun coming up with ideas, brainstorming," he said. "But some of those things are ideas that I wouldn't really care to pursue myself in the first place."

"So this is about being in an environment where you can say ideas without necessarily having to think them through," I said. "The image I have for now is someone who is participating in brainstorming, generating ideas, but even as they generate the ideas, they're putting them in some sort of logical sequence as that's happening so other people can see how it's going to work.

"Being in a role where you can't generate ideas, when you have to follow someone else's game plan, that doesn't necessarily sit well."

"Yeah, that would be me. I couldn't do that."

I told him that while people with high Idea Productivity often frustrate co-workers who have trouble following their zigs and zags, his high Concept Organization would help him put the ideas in a more understandable order.

John was the 90th percentile for Spatial Relations Visualization and in the 30th percentile for Spatial Relations Theory. Given that he worked on the technological side of society rather than the theoretical side, this was hardly surprising. Yet still a major finding!

We then explored his original attraction to computers when he was coming out of high school.

"I didn't know what else to do," he said, "and I knew someone who had gone to the same school and really liked it.

"This was back in 1980, and very few people had even seen a computer except on TV, those little lights blinking and stuff. I always thought of myself as pretty bright, so I thought it was something I could do and be good at and I found out that it was. No one in my family had ever gone to college so I didn't do that."

John's father had been an electronics technician for GE, and "he had a whole electronics set at home. He could fix any radio, that kind of thing."

"Well, this is pretty heavily weighed in terms of genetics," I told him. "This Spatial Relations Visualization, so whatever he had in terms of innate talent, you have. In terms of being able to have that hands-on orientation to make things, to build things, at this point in your career you really don't get to use that much, right?"

"Not as much as I would like."

Although I had no immediate answer to his dilemma, it was obvious that John would be frustrated unless he could find ways to use this ability. I searched for a framework to offer.

I noted that he worked for a large pharmaceutical company. "They make products," I said, "you're just not involved with the direct manufacturing of those products. But there are things you're involved in even if it's just at a distance."

John was in the 65th percentile in Design Memory, which meant he could quickly absorb material through charts, graphs and blueprints. He was in the 85th percentile for Observation.

JOHN'S DISCOVERIES

John heard and was fascinated by his high Idea Productivity, high structural abilities. Suddenly many pieces of his career story came together.

"When you think about this high Observation and high Concept Organization, for instance, you put those together and that's the investigative profile," I said. "This is about someone who looks, goes to the crime scene and can pick up on all kinds of clues, see things and process that information, put them in some sort of logical order to come up with a solution to the problem."

"I knew reading the entire Sherlock Holmes would help me someday."

"There you go," I told him. "And I would go the opposite way in that. I would say that your attraction to Sherlock Holmes was because of how you think and it made sense to you."

John left with several new perspectives on his talents. Usually I alert folks that it takes three to six months to both absorb and use the new "glasses" provided by the Battery and feedback session. I hoped he would put his investigative powers to work and apply his findings.

Takeaways

- **For coaches:** Satisfaction comes from using your abilities and dissatisfaction comes from not being able to use your abilities.
- **For your team:** People with high Idea Productivity often frustrate co-workers who have trouble following their zigs and zags.

LISA'S RESULTS

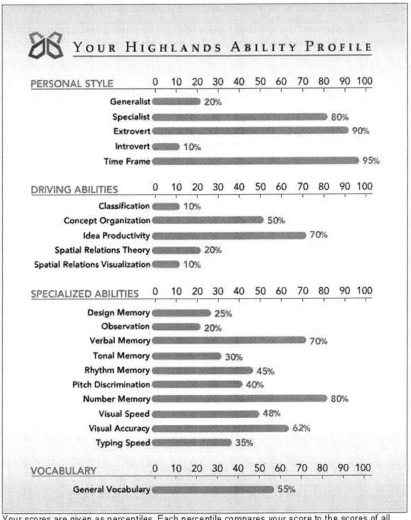

Your scores are given as percentiles. Each percentile compares your score to the scores of all persons who have taken the same worksample.

"The most articulated virtue in Greek culture is Arête. Translated as 'virtue,' the word actually means something close to 'being the best you can be,' or 'reaching your highest human potential'."

— R. Hooker, Wikipedia

XIV. Lisa, 48, Director of Sales
Starting to Plan with Intent

L ike many of the clients I work with, Lisa had chosen her earliest career path mostly by a combination of accident and luck. She has worked very hard to get where she is and is very good at what she does. As a result, she has become financially successful and a recognized leader in her field.

Now she had the chance to start planning for the next phase. She longed to make a big change in the coming years. Now she was ready to think and plan more purposefully about her strengths and how she could best use them. What perfect timing. Here she was approaching the 50s Turning Point with an opportunity to plan her next career!

OUR CONVERSATION

Originally, growing up in Texas, she was going to follow the family tradition and become a teacher. When Lisa graduated and took her first teaching job, a friend of the family told her about a night part-time position opening in marketing with a local theater group. Soon she moved on to a full-time sales position with a national theatre management group and leaving the teaching field altogether.

Lisa took to her sales role immediately: "Talking with customers, finding out their needs, meeting new people, the joy of closing a sale, learning about new businesses, the freedom that came with it, the income that came with it." She spent 10 years in theater management, then joined a global communication/entertainment company in California as a vice president.

I asked Lisa what things came easily to her at work and which required more time, effort or energy.

"I don't enjoy putting numbers together," she said. "I don't like sitting around and calculating. Or statistics. I do it because it's part of my job, but it doesn't come easy to me. I don't enjoy wasting time sitting in long meetings."

What did she like?

"Working with people, developing people, training people, taking on new projects, being the first to take on a new project, anything that has to do with creativity or marketing."

I asked her where she saw herself in five years.

"I don't see myself being in the pace of an environment that I have to be in right now," she said. "I'll be running a medium-sized company, hopefully, or smaller than the one I'm in today."

"Becoming a CEO?"

"CEO or inventing something new, something making a difference in people's lives. I'm a big dreamer, so I'm always planning five or 10 years ahead." She said she could see some of her work at her organization as preparing herself for that next step.

On the Ability Battery, Lisa scored as a Specialist, but I told her, "It's very hard to be in the position that you're in and that kind of organization without having the Generalist footprint.

"There can be smaller units where a manager is a Specialist themselves, but once you get to larger units, you have to have that Generalist perspective. Otherwise it's going to be very, very difficult to figure where people are coming from as well as not having the depth of expertise in a variety of areas. A way to compensate is to surround yourself with a team, a kitchen cabinet, that can provide diverse input."

Lisa also scored as an Extrovert. "I love speaking and performing."

"And selling is performing," I said. "You might not be selling theatre engagement time anymore, but you're selling an idea."

She also had a very high Time Frame, which would draw her to those aspects of her job that would affect her career years down the road, and high Idea Productivity. As an aside, please note how during the interview Lisa mentioned "always planning ahead" – again, the dictum is one cannot not use one's abilities.

Lisa scored low in Classification, which I said put her in fast company – most CEOs and other corporate leaders are low in Classification because, among other things, it often makes it easier to work with people and develop them. "It's much harder to develop other people when you're high in Classification.

"Additionally, this is saying that basically chaotic work situations that are chronic and require rapid problem-solving can be stressful for you. If you were exposed to a role where you had constant chronic ambiguity and had to make decisions without thinking them through, that would be stressful.

"It's really more like being in a situation where there's some tried and true ways of working that you can look at and use."

In Concept Organization, Lisa was mid-range. "This means you can pretty much organize yourself. You're not going to have the downside of procrastination from having to think and analyze it over and over again. There's more of a push towards action, seeing a problem and then jumping on it and moving on.

"So if it's an area where you're an expert, you're talking and leading people and you're working with other people to solve problems in the present, that's energizing and fun." The Extroverted Specialist leader can use her expertise and passion to mobilize others around a vision and lead the way.

Her Idea Productivity was in the 70th percentile, at the edge of high range. She could see evidence of this in her home life.

"My husband is always teasing me because I decide I'm going to write so I become a writer for a while. I mean I always have these ideas. I say that on any given day, I can come up with an idea about this water bottle today and then, in 10 minutes, I can think of another idea for that.

"But I have a lot of projects and ideas that are not totally finished because I got bored with that and went and did something else." The inner life of the high Idea Productivity person is rarely boring!

I told her that the Specialist finding was high enough to influence all aspects of her work life, that she was clearly one who saw things differently.

She had seen this in working with groups: "I'm brainstorming, but rarely am I the person with the final idea."

"That's the key here," I said. "Low Idea Productivity people are the people who are going to follow through." Her high Time Frame, I added, helped her appreciate this more.

Lisa was also low in both areas of Spatial Relations, indicating that she was more comfortable in the world of ideas than in the world of tangible things. She would not have made a good engineer or surgeon.

Among the Specialized Abilities, Lisa scored low in Observation, which I said was probably a good thing for her. High Observation combined with high Idea Productivity like hers can make it very hard to stay focused.

She scored high, 70th percentile, in Verbal Memory. "That's your main Learning Channel," I told her. "It's the one that's reinforced in school. Go home, read the book, talk about the book. So any time you use that you know that's going to stick in your head because that's the strong one for you.

"When you combine that with the extroversion and the Specialist piece....reading is a solitary activity, then the extroversion wants to talk about it."

She had mid-range Rhythm Memory, which fit her being "very, very good, state-level in sports when I was growing up." A lot of this probably had been due to her competitive nature. Here again her Specialist finding and her high Grip come into play.

"I'm just an average person with a lot of drive and determination and that's it," she said.

I was momentarily taken aback by this self-summary. "Well, to tell you the truth I really don't know what average is," I told her.

"I'm saying that there's a fascinating and powerful combination in terms of being an out-of-the-box thinker, having ideas, being able to put them out there, getting up in front of people, having enough charisma to draw them with you into a vision that you can picture a long time ahead, and the willingness not to get frustrated and keep going towards that vision.

"It's also about your being able to pick people to complement you and put them in roles where they can feel successful. I think those are your talents. I'm just not willing to boil it down to 'I'm an average person.'"

One talent Lisa clearly has was in Number Memory, and I told her, "It's good to be a woman in a company who doesn't have anxiety when they see numbers. A woman who can show up and not be intimidated by numbers, that's a big thing.

"It doesn't bring you any joy, necessarily, but it's not a stressful activity for you."

LISA'S DISCOVERIES

I think the largest discovery was my challenge to her view of herself as being "just an average person" And that was a turning point in the discussion. Her focus on being a Specialist/Extrovert as well and having high Idea Productivity coupled with her experiential problem-solving and decision-making style fed her passion (Specialist) and made her a "natural" in developing others.

Lisa and I then discussed ways to use what she had learned and various types of work that best used her abilities.

"I would say that it takes anywhere between three and four months for a person to internalize the results of this to the point that they think of themselves in certain ways," I told her. Then you almost "brainwash" the people around you to think of you in certain ways.

"You understand how you can come up with a lot of ideas in a short period of time and you start referring to yourself that way and eventually your boss or your colleagues pick up on that.

"When that happens you've got a victory because you're more likely to be put in roles where you'll be successful."

Takeaways

- **For you:** Worth repeating, even with the double negative: One cannot not use one's abilities.
- **For coaches:** A Creative Specialist finding shapes the rest of the results regardless of scores.
- **For coaches:** There is no such thing as an "average person." Each of us is a unique combination of the Eight Factors.
- **For teams:** Leaders who are Extroverted Specialists lead others through their own expertise, passion and high levels of interactive communication. These leaders 'sell' a vision of a better future.

TAKSHEEL'S RESULTS

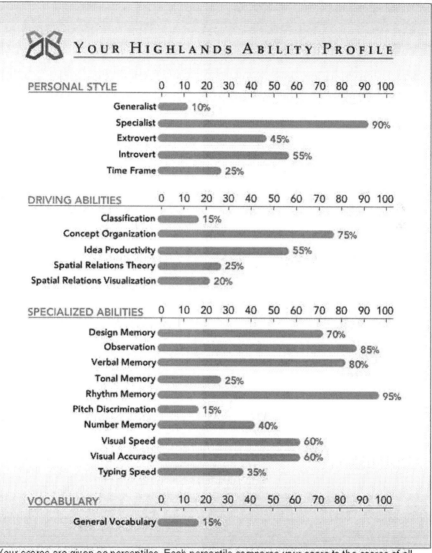

YOUR HIGHLANDS ABILITY PROFILE

PERSONAL STYLE — 0 10 20 30 40 50 60 70 80 90 100

- Generalist 10%
- Specialist 90%
- Extrovert 45%
- Introvert 55%
- Time Frame 25%

DRIVING ABILITIES — 0 10 20 30 40 50 60 70 80 90 100

- Classification 15%
- Concept Organization 75%
- Idea Productivity 55%
- Spatial Relations Theory 25%
- Spatial Relations Visualization 20%

SPECIALIZED ABILITIES — 0 10 20 30 40 50 60 70 80 90 100

- Design Memory 70%
- Observation 85%
- Verbal Memory 80%
- Tonal Memory 25%
- Rhythm Memory 95%
- Pitch Discrimination 15%
- Number Memory 40%
- Visual Speed 60%
- Visual Accuracy 60%
- Typing Speed 35%

VOCABULARY — 0 10 20 30 40 50 60 70 80 90 100

- General Vocabulary 15%

Your scores are given as percentiles. Each percentile compares your score to the scores of all persons who have taken the same worksample.

"The North Wind and the Sun disputed as to which was the most powerful, and agreed that he should be declared the victor who could first strip a wayfaring man of his clothes. The North Wind first tried his power and blew with all his might, but the keener his blasts, the closer the Traveler wrapped his cloak around him, until at last, resigning all hope of victory, the Wind called upon the Sun to see what he could do. The Sun suddenly shone out with all his warmth. The Traveler no sooner felt his genial rays than he took off one garment after another, and at last, fairly overcome with heat, undressed and bathed in a stream that lay in his path."

— Aesop's Fables

XV. Taksheel, 53, Senior Manager, Pharmaceuticals
The Entrepreneurial Profile

Those of us who use this Battery in combination with the Whole Person or Eight Factor models often discuss the transferability of our work to other cultures. In the past 15 years, we have found these tools, especially the Battery, helpful in our work with global scientists and leaders. Since English is still the standard language of business around the globe, the Ability Battery works quite well (with some slight modifications).

But almost equally significant is the exploration of the Eight Factors, especially the Family of Origin and its impact on each of us. Your Abilities become you in the present while your Family of Origin puts you and your choices into your personal story, enriched by knowing your abilities.

OUR CONVERSATION

Taksheel is a manager with a large pharmaceutical company, with about 10 people working for him.

He is a 53-year-old native of India who came to the U.S. for his higher education and got his Ph.D. in organic chemistry.

He grew up in a rural area. His mother had a seventh-grade education, and his father was a high school dropout. English is his second language. His earlier study was in the local language.

He said he was always good in science and math, "and the family kind of influenced me to go to medical school, although I was always very mechanical in terms of working with my hands and all that."

He went to a large state university and ended up studying organic chemistry because he was interested in the pharmaceutical industry.

"I finished my Ph.D. in five years," he said. "And in the first three years, my main goal was to avoid getting kicked out of the program. I couldn't imagine going back under those circumstances.

"I can see now that I could have had a breakdown due to stress my first year in school with trying to adapt to the English language, cultural differences, missing my family.

"But I always had a good stress management system, I guess, inherently. Partly because I grew up in a family where my father had a lot of problems, health-wise, and being the eldest son I had to bear a lot of the responsibility."

I couldn't help but reflect on how important Family of Origin influences were on Taksheel as he pursued his career. It was easier to see in someone from a society where family traditionally plays a larger role than in the U.S. However, it is vital here as well, something I encourage my clients to weigh carefully along with their results in the Ability Battery.

In my own life, I don't do anything that resembles what my parents or grandparents did. We were all furriers, barbers, guerrillas, entrepreneurial small business owners in Greece and the U.S. What

I know and can see is that how I do my work is impacted greatly by this past. And this past becomes more obvious when we are under perceived stress. It is at those times our Family of Origin and the past relationships impact how we respond and what we see.

After finishing postdoctoral work at a fairly prestigious university, Taksheel took a job in the pharmaceutical industry in the area of drug development – optimizing what had already been discovered. He would have preferred work in discovering new drugs, but there was a recession and he found that these opportunities were going to graduates of the more prestigious schools – Harvard, MIT or Stanford, for example.

"The opportunities for development, publication, patenting, etc. were very limited," he said. "And to tell you honestly, the job satisfaction was quite low."

He said that this was partly due to the limited chances to problem-solve and that after five years, he moved to the area of regulatory affairs. Three years later, he moved to a smaller company. He also got his M.B.A. and got particular enjoyment out of his marketing and statistics courses.

"I do believe I have a little entrepreneurial gene in me," he said. "I think in some respects I'm a risk-taker. I never thought about staying in one place for security and stability."

Taksheel then moved again, to his current position with the pharmaceutical company after a family friend arranged an interview there.

"How did you feel about the transition from lab scientist to manager?" I asked him.

"It was a slow progression," he said. "I still feel I'm good in the lab with my hands. Now I don't do lab science, but I work with scientists. Managing people isn't an issue with me. But in our management system, we have the responsibility without the authority and that is stressful."

He was also stressed by the commute for the job – he was living hundreds of miles away – so he moved back to his family and took a job with a pharmaceutical firm as senior director of regulatory affairs. "I'm kind of a liaison person with the FDA on manufacturing aspects of the drug and quality control. I like smaller companies because there is less bureaucracy. Everyone knows everyone.

"Even now sometimes I get big pharmaceutical opportunities and I tell myself, 'You know, that's not for me.'" The company had been trying to keep him interested by offering him some project management roles, but he was thinking it was time to strike out on his own.

"Oh, I could be a vice president and probably make a few thousand dollars more, but if I do something entrepreneurial and it pans out even 50 percent, I will be a lot more happy and closer to my true goal than with the title and career. This entrepreneurial itch is not going to leave me, and I would only regret not trying it."

Taksheel was clearly a Specialist, ranking in the 90th percentile. "This doesn't mean that Specialists can't manage people," I told him, "it's just that it's harder to manage others who also are not Specialists. A Specialist managing a group of Generalists would be very difficult, but managing other scientists who are also experts, that's different."

I noted that Specialist/Generalist conflicts are quite common in organizations "in the sense that Generalists want to know just enough that they can get by and the Specialist wants to understand everything about how the system works and assumes everyone else wants that, too."

Taksheel's Specialist personality was well suited to being an entrepreneur, I explained, because "having control is important for the Specialist in terms of having control of the outcome of the product."

On the Introvert/Extrovert scale, Taksheel came out in the middle, what we sometimes call an "ambivert."

"You're probably a little bit more on the Introvert side," I told him, but in terms of being able to connect to people, to talk to people, to get energy from people from the Extrovert world, you can be on that side of the world, you just can't stay there for very long.

"Going from meeting to meeting during the daytime and interacting with different groups of people would be pretty exhausting for someone like yourself if you had to do it on a regular basis."

"I don't disagree."

"So having some period where you can kind of go into your own world, think things through and then come out reenergized is one way to regulate your own energy during the day."

By being in the middle of the Extrovert/Introvert scale, I told him, he could function both as a Specialist/Extrovert who liked to demonstrate his expertise to people and as a Specialist/Introvert, the inwardly focused scientist. "They don't mind the hours of being by themselves because they don't need other people necessarily to confirm or validate their thinking.

"You could sell people on an idea if you feel really passionate about it. It's just that if you do it too much, you get exhausted."

But he'd have to be really passionate about it, I added. "For a Generalist, that might not be necessary. For you, it is."

Taksheel scored low on Time Frame. I told him that this would not stand in the way of his developing a business but that he would have to be aware of it.

"Long-range problem planning could be a challenge," I said. "People who are low Time Frame need to plan, let's say in six- to 12-month increments and then build a plan based on that so they can go out three years.

"So if you were to create a business plan, for instance, you might want to think about, 'OK, in six months from now, we will know where we are. In 12 months, where do we want to be? In 18 months?' That way it's much more tangible than just saying, 'OK, let's do a five-year business plan.'"

This fit well with Taksheel's assessment of himself. He didn't want to stay with his current company, he said, "because it's not going to take me to a stage where I want to be in the time frame I want to be there. I'm 53 and I want to do this before I'm 70. Their sense of urgency is very different from my sense of urgency.

"I saw a situation where it took them two months to get the data, and I was pushing and pushing, but I was the only one pushing. That's the frustration I kind of go through."

I then gave Taksheel the advice I generally give someone trying to develop a company or a team: Choose people who complement your skills rather than duplicate them.

"Would it be helpful," I asked him, "especially when you go out on your own to be able to include in your company somebody who has a more long-term Time Frame? Someone who can help you think strategically, OK?

"It could even be an unpaid group of people who you take out to dinner every three months and say, 'Here's what I'm doing, give me your honest feedback.'"

Taksheel scored low in Classification, which I explained made it easy for him to listen to other people and use past experience to solve problems. Not surprisingly for someone with his background – and career choice – he scored much higher on Concept Organization.

"This could be the person who takes a proposal through FDA approval and edits it so it flows, so that it can be understood in a step-by-step manner. The project manager in an organization is often someone with high Concept Organization.

"Any task that requires you to do that kind of thinking is fun and relatively stress-free for you, so this is your main problem-solving decision-making ability. The downside of it can be procrastination in the sense that you double-check yourself to make sure you went through all the steps correctly. One way around that is to create artificial deadlines for yourself."

In Idea Productivity, Taksheel scored in the 55th percentile, the upper end of mid-range. Although this meant he generated a fairly large number of ideas when presented with a problem, he said his colleagues were often unaware of this because he needed to process the ideas before discussing them.

"Many times what happens is I walk out of a meeting and within an hour I have one answer or another."

I told him that it might be good to know as much as possible what particular problem might be coming up in a meeting so he could brainstorm as much as possible.

All told, I said, "you have a nice combination of being analytical, high Concept Organization, generating ideas, seeing things differently and being action-oriented."

He scored low in both areas of Spatial Relations, which showed his preference for functioning in the abstract world. He had told me earlier in the session that he had once considered law school or business school, which would have made sense given this aspect of his ability profile.

"I'm good in science and working in the lab," said, "but I have no qualms moving out of it. You might have the best scientists, but they have to be motivated. The HR part of it, people being motivated and motivating them, these kinds of things I take to heart, you know?"

"In terms of moving in that entrepreneurial area, "I told him, "it's going to be more helpful than being in the structural world."

Among the Specialized Abilities, what stood out was Taksheel's 95th percentile score in Rhythm Memory.

"People who have high Rhythm Memory are people who are very active," I said. "They have lots of energy, they're constantly moving. It's hard for them to sit behind a computer all day long and sit still. When they move around, they get freed up to solve problems. And they get energy from that movement."

I asked him if he did any kind of physical exercise.

"Yes, I do. I try to work out every day, but at least four or five days a week."

"For you, working out may not be as much a choice as a necessity. Moreover, you want to keep in mind that you learn through muscle memory, through movement and observing movements. Here's a powerful way for you to learn new things."

He had told me he liked to fix things around his house, which I explained had less to do with being in the structural world and more about learning through doing.

Taksheel also had a high score in Observation, which meant he could read people easily by watching their body language, work with draftsmen or architects or walk into a plant and sense quickly what was going on. He scored high in Verbal Memory, which meant he could easily absorb knowledge through reading, and in Design Memory, the ability to translate visual patterns into the written or spoken word.

He mentioned that he took notes when reading, which I explained was not just an aid to memorizing but a way of memorizing: The very act of doing so made him more likely to recall the material.

"People unconsciously find ways to adjust to their Learning Channels, they just aren't doing it purposefully," I said. "When you write something down, it's easier for you to take it in.

"So you have three ways of learning new things fast. The writing it down, the reading it, and then being able to see it in a picture or even draw a picture for yourself when someone has a design. Given a new experience, you can take in information pretty quickly.

"But if you have high Learning Channels, you have to use them. It can't be the same old thing."

Taksheel scored low in two other areas, Pitch Discrimination and Vocabulary, but I told him not to be concerned about either one. He wasn't going to be a musician, and English wasn't his first language. Having used the Battery with English-speaking professionals, especially scientists internationally, I often find that that their Vocabulary scores are in the lower percentiles.

I justify the use of the Vocabulary section in that all of the companies I have worked with – even if they are global – have English as their language of business. Also with Vocabulary, we are not measuring the specialized jargon of a professional but rather his subtle understanding of the meaning of words.

Taksheel clearly had been able to communicate with me, I told him, "and my guess is you don't experience that as an issue in your job, either." Plus with his specialized vocabulary – the language of pharmaceuticals – he was not at a disadvantage. "Improving your vocabulary isn't a bad idea," I told him, "but by just hanging around with your sons you're going to pick up on more vocabulary words, anyway." After all, Arnold Schwarzenegger learned English through TV soaps!

TAKSHEEL'S DISCOVERIES

What registered for Taksheel was being able to frame his concerns about his otherwise successful career into a language of strength. Moreover, the question of going forward was not about abilities but rather coming up with a plan and building a team for himself. His low Time Frame and high Grip score bode well for his success, especially with the right people.

Can Taksheel take the risk? Should he? The answers don't lie completely in his Ability profile, as there is nothing in the results that says you can't do something. It's more pointing out your strengths and challenges. Equally significant in his case are his Family of Origin and the themes expressed over past generations. Having an articulated awareness of your real talents can be the difference between success and failure as a leader. You need to see both the interplay among them and also how they relate to those of others on your team.

Over the years, I have worked with countless scientists who were being placed in managerial roles, This is a perfect example of how the abilities that made you good at an area don't necessarily work easily and as well in a different role. Going from being an individual contributor to working through others to get work done is a significant leap. And then that leap gets more challenging as one who is a Specialist and structural person gets more distant from hands-on work and has to do more work through others.

Takeaways

- **For coaches:** The Ability Battery generally works well with people from other cultures, although their Vocabulary scores are of course likely to be lower if their native language is not English.
- **For you:** If you're starting a new company, be sure to actively seek out and consult people with different abilities, even if on an informal basis.

Detour: Two Clients Speak on Family of Origin

June, 36 "I interviewed my mother this evening, which was amazing. I learned stuff I didn't know about her and her father. I am not finished yet, but so far, very good. The more interesting thing was how she seemed to have such energy and clarity when she spoke – the interaction was far more enjoyable to me than if we were to simply have a normal conversation. She became someone who I had an increased respect for. She always plays such a one down position, when in fact she is tough as nails and very competent."

Kate, 41 "Many insights have been gained from doing the family interview. I have had the opportunity to see things in a whole different light. Without processing all the 'pieces,' I really believed that work was merely a means to an end – to meet financial needs and to ensure security – for my maternal grandfather. I knew he worked on a boiler at a dog food company all of my life and that he had not gone to college. As a matter of fact, he only completed the eighth grade.

"What I didn't know was that he was licensed by the government and had to be tested and re-licensed annually. When looking back, I remember several things: He was always drawing, measuring and creating. I remember pieces of paper around the house that I assumed were just doodles everywhere. He could fix anything and was a wizard with tools. He enjoyed what he did – I know this because he attempted to teach me everything about using tools. He was actually using training, experience, skills and probably natural ability to complete his work. I also remember him fixing neighbors' heaters and working on the plumbing and other building projects at our church.

"Lo and behold...my grandfather had a career. He was rarely ever, to my recollection, absent from work. Clichéd as it may sound, my grandfather probably 'lived to work.'

"Through this process, it was also necessary for me reframe my concept of education. Career-related education does not always equate with college. I could have saved myself a lot of embarrassment if I had reframed this earlier in life. I can be a real superficial jerk sometimes."

PETER'S RESULTS

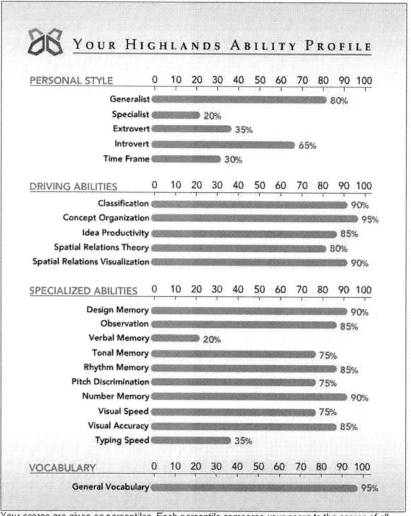

Your scores are given as percentiles. Each percentile compares your score to the scores of all persons who have taken the same worksample.

"Craving, which leads to rebirth."
— The Pali Canon (sacred Buddhist scripture)

XVI. Peter, 55, Credit Manager
When Nothing in Your Company Works

Consider that upon taking the bend of age 50 and starting to see the final laps, one can be swept up in the desire, the need, to set a course – a way to contribute, to be productive, be valued and give back through mentoring and coaching the next generation.

However, you also are quite aware that at least one more career is in you and you want to make that a reality. Instead of heading toward diminished powers, here one can launch oneself forward in a realistic way.

OUR CONVERSATION

Peter, 55, is one of seven credit managers at a pharmaceutical-related company. He came into the consulting room full of enthusiasm, his hands and eyes brimming with energy and his verbal fluency almost dominating the initial interview. Peter was determined to take advantage of his time with me and get the most out of it for himself and to work on a plan for his career!

In college, he liked electronics and considered being a physics major. He eventually wound up majoring in engineering and going to work for defense contractors and also getting his M.B.A. His company was bought by a major defense contractor, and he was laid off. He worked briefly for a smaller company and then was hired by a large pharmaceutical company, moving to the financial planning side.

He had been with his current employer for the past seven years.

"I ended up as a credit manager here and I don't like credit," he said. "I'm not a confrontational, contentious person, and credit is inherently confrontational and contentious. That's not me, but they needed someone who could set up a credit system because there was none before, and I wrote our entire credit system. It's a monster spreadsheet, but it does everything you could ask in a credit system and I love programming.

"One of the hardest things I've had to do was when I hired our second person here. I hired a technical person, and he was the only one who could pass my Excel test. I had to step back, but it does take me away from my fun stuff."

I asked Peter what he saw himself doing in five or 10 years.

"I don't know of any job in this company that would work," he said. "I haven't given up, but I haven't found anything yet. I love analysis work, I love creating, I love to do things. I like to do things as against lead people. I don't think of myself as a natural-born leader. One of the hardest things is for me to delegate."

As a Generalist, one might have thought Peter would have no problem delegating. But the Ability Battery is really the interplay of the various factors, I explained, and "there are going to be things that might be contradicted by another finding."

Peter also scored high as an Introvert, 65th percentile, but said that "over time, my life has required me to be more extroverted and so I've grown into that some more." This section of the Battery, given its self-report nature (e.g., What would you rather do at a party? Talk to many or a few, etc.), is influenced by your perception of your work setting, context, poor recall and desire to please or to present oneself in a desirable light.

"With my wife," he recalled, "when I was dating her, her family basically said, 'If you're going to be part of this family, you have to learn how to help out with these parties and things,' because they were an extrovert family.

"At business school, the way to success is have your hand up and participate in class. That was not me, but I said, 'I can do this. Nobody knows me. I can be someone else here.' So I did it.

"I got called on in the second class and said something and liter- ally when the words stopped flowing out of my lips, I could not even remember what I had said. My heart was racing, but I looked around and no one was laughing and no one was staring at me, and I said, 'OK. That worked. That worked. I can do this again.'"

I told him that in a team environment, an introverted Generalist can be "objective and neutral and almost detached. You can be team-oriented and still keep your own counsel, essentially."

In terms of Time Frame, Peter thought of himself as long-range planner, always considering consequences down the road. But he scored fairly low in Time Frame. It isn't often we find such a difference between a person's experience of themselves and the results.

I am always interested in digging further because often times this is fascinating and can also clarify a likely confusion between personal career planning and requirements of a job role.

In Peter's case, it was more about being strong in Concept Organization and enjoying planning and being systematic as opposed to immediately thinking ahead of the consequences of a decision.

"When you think in terms of personal career planning," I asked him, "how far ahead do you think?"

"I always hope that my job will be the last or my current company will be the last one," he said. "I've found that I get an itch after three years. I can hang in there for a while and then I get really antsy in five or so."

"My first jobs, my first two programming assignments, were exactly that – to fix broken things and move on to the next project. Here's a program, it does this, it doesn't work, fix it, and oh, by the way, here's the one comment line, take this programming language and fix it ... I love it, I love that sort of thing."

"You have this drive for results," I said. What I know is that a client, given the time to talk about how he works, will end up validating for himself what his abilities are. However, to organize the data can only take place with a semi-objective outsider like a trained coach. Additionally, if you recall my initial description of Peter, his actions and attitude support the low Time Frame result!

In Classification, Peter had the high score of people who thrive in fast-paced environments. "The more ambiguous a solution, the more novelty involved, the more fun it is in terms of solving problems," I told him. "Novelty is the key word there."

"The way I look at it for me," he said, "is that I like a reasonably fast pace. I don't like to reach the hectic stage, but when it gets chaotic, I don't find it fun anymore."

"Hectic is different from having novel problems to solve," I said.

Peter's high Classification explained the difficulty he had in delegating. "It's hard to delegate new problems to someone else when they're so satisfying for you to solve them," I said. "It's easier to develop people when you're low in Classification. You're more patient."

"Yes, if I hand something off, it takes three times as long," he said. Here we find the usual perception held by the high Classification person. It is easy to see how working through others to get things done – the management role – takes skills that go against the high Classification grain.

Peter was also high in Concept Organization, 95th percentile, which actually helped him think long term. "This is the one that says, 'OK, let's think of this project and work backwards or work forwards and see where it's going to take us,'" I said.

"Well, I'm always thinking about the most critical path," he said. "I mean to get to such and such on time, we have to do this first, and this, and this, and this, and you've got to do these steps…and it always just frustrates me that my wife is terrible with time management."

"Likely she's low Concept Organization," I said.

"Yeah, and she's very neat and organized, and my room is messy."

"There's your example right there," I said. "Low Concept Organization people need the external world to organize them; high Concept Organization people don't. The low Concept people have the neater work space because they work at it."

With his high scores in both Classification and Concept Organization, Peter fit the profile of a "consultative problem-solver," someone who "thrives in situations where they get to come in, identify the flaws and then tell people the steps they need to take to fix them. And then moves on to the next problem."

"I always thought I would be great as a consultant."

"Well, that's exactly what we're talking about, that combination of abilities," I said.

Peter was high in Idea Productivity, Spatial Relations Theory and Spatial Relations Visualization – the other three Driving Abilities. I explained how this can be a mixed blessing.

"That's the multi-ability profile, so finding a job that's going to satisfy all these Drivers simultaneously will be very difficult. You have a problem of overabundance. You've got a lot of stuff going on and talents and abilities that need to be used."

High Idea Productivity can lead to problems with focus and follow-through, and we agreed that this was an area in which Peter could work harder by understanding his strengths, "teaching you to educate the person you report to how best to utilize you."

"That would be good."

"That's the point. I think it's brainwashing people around us so they can start thinking about us in a way that maximizes our contribution. Because you're someone who can be this tremendous problem-solver and generate ideas. It could mean being the adviser to the boss behind the scenes where they kind of bounce ideas off you and you process with them. That's an interesting role if you think about it."

"I could enjoy something like that," he said. "I would say I'm a behind-the-scenes guy. I don't need to be out front. The recognition stuff is nice, really nice, but on a day-to-day basis, I don't have to have people knowing me."

Peter's high scores in both aspects of Spatial Relations meant he was highly comfortable in both the concrete and theoretical worlds, which as a Generalist could pull him in different career directions. "You said that programming is a fun thing for you, but now you're having to work more through others."

"Yes, I'm giving away fun stuff, but I have to do it. It's part of my job."

Peter clearly had to have some outlet in the structural world. He had once found it through home improvement projects, but seemed to have little time for this anymore.

"Well, at some point, the scientist who's no longer working in the lab might be involved with a team that does work in the lab and that might be satisfying enough," I said. "They're not so disconnected that they become what they perceive.

"People in the structural world see people who work purely as managers as meaningless. It's not really work, they push papers around. They're not really creating something that you can see and feel."

"I used to say the role of manager is to run interference so the real people can get the real work done," he said.

Peter's visual abilities, Design Memory and Observation, also were high. I told him that the latter can be particularly helpful in persuading people in that he can quickly sense when he isn't convincing them and change course.

His Verbal Memory was low, but his Musical Abilities were generally high, one more indication that he'd need to find outlets in the hands-on structural world, either at work or away from it.

Peter's Vocabulary score was 95th percentile, and it led us to a brief discussion of his goals and values.

"We think that people who score like you do should aim high in their careers," I said, "because we see folks at the highest levels of Vocabulary within their professions such as CEOs of global companies, grad school professors, attorneys and above – folks at top of their professions."

Peter's first marriage ended in divorce when he was completing business school. "I was ready to hit the road running and sort of conquer the road, although I wasn't a really pushy, skyrocket-type person.

"But from then on, I just realized family was so important to me.

"Aiming high also means time away from your family, and when you come down to it, what do you get? You get more money and no time to spend it because you're not with your family anymore.

"So that's why I value being able to leave at 5:00. I did leave at 8:00 the other night and I've had a few 6:00s and 7:00s recently, but the norm is I leave at 5:00 The good pay and great work-life balance are the reasons I've been able to hang in there despite not enjoying the job itself."

"Yes," I said, "that's why we say that the abilities form the foundation, but that's where these other things come in."

"That's one of the frustrations for me with the abilities I have," he said. "You mentioned consulting. I'd love consulting, but consulting for one of the big firms means you sell your soul to the company, you just travel. I would actually enjoy some travel right now, and with the kids older, my wife wouldn't mind me being away from the house a little more, but I wouldn't want to be away five days a week on a regular basis.

"The company I'm with now is a good company, but I'm tired of my job. My title says 'manager,' but I'm not really a manager. But my job is a lot more stressful than some of the managers'. I've thought about a lateral move, but I'd really need more specialized skills for that."

PETER'S DISCOVERIES

The multiple Drivers – high Classification, high Concept Organization, high Idea Productivity and being in the structural (the tangible side) world – that Peter brings to situations along with verbal abilities (high Vocabulary) make for a powerful combination. Seeing his abilities confirmed for Peter what he could contribute.

With this combination, Peter and people like him will struggle in many ways, as satisfaction on a regular basis is difficult. At the most basic level, Peter needs to translate his abilities into simple sentences and educate his boss – that's what I mean by brainwashing – to understand and "use" Peter more productively.

Having multiple abilities does not necessarily make for an easy work life! This is why we don't just look at abilities but also use the other factors as keys for leading a successful and productive life.

Takeaways

- **For teams:** In a team environment, an introverted Generalist can be objective and neutral and almost detached. He can be team-oriented and still keep his own counsel, essentially.
- **For coaches:** Despite their wealth of talents, clients with a multi-ability profile present a particular challenge in finding a job that will satisfy all their Drivers.
- **For you:** high Observation can be particularly helpful in persuading people because you can quickly sense when you are not convincing them and change course.

PART 3

TEST DRIVES: ASSESSMENT AND THOUGHT EXERCISES

I n this section, I will give the reader a chance to discover some of the insights my clients discovered about themselves in their case studies.

I will briefly provide a number of exercises, each built around one of the career factors mentioned in my client sessions, i.e., Abilities, Family of Origin and Career Development Cycle. Of course, there are additional factors, but these will have to wait until the completion of my next book – in progress as you read this one. If you are interested in viewing complete sample Ability Reports for Students, Adults and Leaders please visit me at www.imdleadership.com

* * *

APPLICATION EXERCISE 1: CAREER DEVELOPMENT

Draw on a single sheet of poster paper a pictorial representation of a time line that gives relative positions to all of your jobs to date. Start with your first one – paid or unpaid – and continue until the present.

Once you have completed your time line and work history, extend them five years into the future and consider what role you would like to have at that time, what skills and abilities you will need in that role, and in what environment you will be using them.

When you have positioned all your jobs, review your thoughts and your data. What made you decide on the role? What other roles drew you? What turning points did you encounter and what made you aware of them? How did your family of origin influence you? How did your friends influence you? What roles did you identify as the best matches for your abilities?

_____

_____

_____

_____

_____

Example of a Time Line represented linearly:

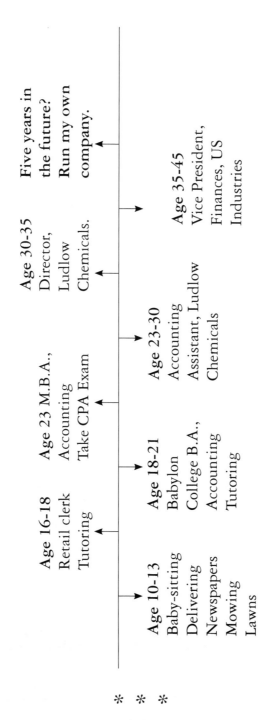

Age 10-13
Baby-sitting
Delivering
Newspapers
Mowing
Lawns

Age 16-18
Retail clerk
Tutoring

Age 18-21
Babylon
College B.A.,
Accounting
Tutoring

Age 23 M.B.A.,
Accounting
Take CPA Exam

Age 23-30
Accounting
Assistant, Ludlow
Chemicals

Age 30-35
Director,
Ludlow
Chemicals.

Age 35-45
Vice President,
Finances, US
Industries

Five years in
the future?
Run my own
company.

* * *

APPLICATION EXERCISE 2:
ABILITY SELF-REPORT

This exercise will give you a sense of elements of your Personal Work Style, as well as key Drivers in your decision-making and problem-solving style, i.e., the ways in which you interact with others and how you engage problems and decisions.

We have found that where abilities are involved, self-report assessments are far less helpful than objective assessments in defining these elements. Many instruments on the market today, including Myers-Briggs, require the test-taker to self-report. In so doing, they ignore the natural tendency of test-takers to present themselves in the best light possible: the person they'd like to be, or who will be most impressive to the reader – a current or prospective employer, perhaps.

By definition, in self-reporting you choose among preferences – your own or those of the person who views your results – not on the objective performance of work samples, which produce measurable results. The process of self-reporting forces you to assess yourself. And as I have seen from experiments in my graduate courses at Saint Joseph's University in Philadelphia, people who assess their own natural abilities are wrong about two-thirds of the time! In test-taking, as in life, our ability to deceive ourselves is almost limitless.

Think of the taking this self-report as a sample of Highlands Battery much as a trip through a virtual college. Completing the actual Battery and working with a coach to analyze the results is like enrolling and completing your freshman year. Working with the coach over a sustained period to develop a Personal Vision is like earning a college degree!

This exercise is designed to help you make a reasonable determination of the position you will occupy on continuums measured by high, medium and low among only some of the key abilities measured by the Highlands Ability Battery.

Read over the earlier sections of this book that discuss Generalist and Specialist. Then observe your actions and activities for a week and look back over the past several weeks. Try to recall whether you acted as an expert drilling deep-down into a subject or a jack-of-all-trades interested in everything. Note your level of satisfaction in your various work roles.

It's impossible to determine a person's abilities by observing her behavior. The same behavior in different people may be the result of different constellations of high and low abilities. This is why the Ability Battery works so well; it differentiates abilities by isolating each one.

Remember that everyone – especially those among us who are most competitive – wants and expects to rank high in everything.

But this isn't Lake Wobegon, where everyone is above average –or has a need to be. How you approach a problem has very little to do with your I.Q.

Here are the characteristics that distinguish high and low performers in various natural abilities. Place a check mark alongside the statements that describe you best. In some cases, your selections may appear to be inconsistent; in most cases, not.

STRONG GENERALIST	STRONG SPECIALIST
1. TEAM PLAYER, WORKS WITH OTHERS	**1.** MAY TRY TO IMPOSE OWN STANDARDS ON GROUP
2. PREFERS A VARIETY OF TASKS	**2.** ENJOYS PERFECTING ONE SPECIFIC TASK
3. TENDS TO SHARE A COMMON VIEW	**3.** HAS A UNIQUE PERSPECTIVE INTENSE AND PASSIONATE
4. FOCUSES ON GROUP GOALS	**4.** PREFERS INDIVIDUAL ASSIGNMENTS
5. FINDS IT EASY TO DELEGATE, DOESN T NEED TO BE AN EXPERT	**5.** NEEDS TO BE THE EXPERT, FINDS IT HARDER TO DELEGATE
6. JACK-OF-ALL-TRADES MIND-SET	**6.** WANTS TO BE THE GO-TO PERSON IN A SPECIFIC AREA OF KNOWLEDGE OR PERFORMANCE
7. WORKS WELL IN LARGE ORGANIZATIONS	**7.** CHALLENGED BY WORKING IN A LARGE BUREAUCRATIC ORGANIZATION
8. FINDS IT EASY TO BE UNDERSTOOD	**8.** MORE LIKELY TO FEEL MISUNDERSTOOD
9. ENJOYS A FAST-PACED ENVIRONMENT WITH MULTIPLE DEMANDS AND ROLES	**9.** LIKES TO CONCENTRATE ON AND UNDERSTAND AREA IN DEPTH

Pick the choice below that appears to identify you best and write a brief paragraph based on your general reading and this "self-report."

I appear to be a strong Generalist. That means

_____

....

....

I appear to be a Specialist/Generalist. That means

_____

....

....

I appear to be a Specialist. That means

_____

....

....

EXTROVERSION	INTROVERSION
1. NEEDS INTERACTION WITH OTHERS	**1.** WORKS BEST ALONE
2. INTERACTION IS A REWARD IN ITSELF	**2.** INTERACTS WHEN NECESSARY, PREFERS STRUCTURE IN RELATIONSHIPS
3. FEELS STRESS WORKING ALONE	**3.** FEELS ENERGY DRAIN AFTER INTERACTION

EXTROVERSION	INTROVERSION
4. THINKS BEST AFTER FEEDBACK FROM OTHERS	**4.** DEVELOPS THOUGHTS THROUGH REFLECTION
5. TALKING ALOUD HELPS UNDERSTANDING	**5.** PREFERS QUIET EXCHANGES
6. ENJOYS INTERACTING FOR ITS OWN SAKE	**6.** INTERACTS WITH EFFORT
7. TALKS FIRST, THEN THINKS	**7.** THINKS, THEN SPEAKS
8. SHARES THOUGHTS EASILY AND SPONTANEOUSLY	**8.** KEEPS THOUGHTS UNTIL WELL FORMED

Pick the choice below that appears to identify you best and write a brief paragraph based on your general reading and your entries.

I appear to be a strong Extrovert. That means

_____

....

....

I appear to be an Ambivert. That means

_____

....

....

I appear to be an Introvert. That means

_____

....

....

TIME FRAME – LOW	TIME FRAME – HIGH
1. MOVES EASILY FROM PROJECT TO PROJECT	**1.** PREFERS TO FOCUS ON LONGER-TERM PROJECTS
2. EASILY ORGANIZES AND COMPLETES PROJECTS REQUIRING ONE YEAR OR LESS	**2.** LOOKS INTO THE LONGER-TERM FUTURE FOR PLANS AND GOALS
3. CAN ACHIEVE LONG-TERM GOALS BY BREAKING THEM INTO SHORT-TERM PROJECTS	**3.** CAN HELP AN ORGANIZATION FIND IMPETUS FOR LONG-RANGE PLANNING
4. HUNGERS FOR SHORT-TERM RESULTS	**4.** CAN PUT OFF GRATIFICATION AND REWARDS UNTIL LONG-TERM GOAL IS REACHED
5. PULL TO TACTICAL CHANGES, NEW WORK PROCESSES, A HIGHER SALES GOAL	**5.** PULL TO STRATEGIC CHANGES, CREATING A NEW VISION OR NEW CULTURE FOR AN ORGANIZATION. VERIFY THAT CURRENT PROJECTS ARE CONSISTENT WITH LONG-TERM GOALS
6. FULFILLS FIREFIGHTER S ROLE IN AN ORGANIZATION, THRIVES ON PUTTING OUT FIRES	**6.** BECOMES STRESSED IN FIREFIGHTING ROLES.
7. RESULTS-DRIVEN, RESPONDS TO IMMEDIATE PROBLEMS	**7.** MAY LOSE SIGHT OF SHORT-TERM STEPS TO LONG-TERM GOAL

TIME FRAME – LOW	TIME FRAME – HIGH
8. MAY SAY, HOW CAN I PLAN AHEAD 3-5 YEARS WHEN THINGS CHANGE SO MUCH DAY TODAY?	**8.** MAY MISS OPPORTUNITIES IN THE NEAR TERM WITH THEIR FOCUS ON THE LONGER TERM. MAY SAY, HOW CAN WE ACCOMPLISH OUR GOALS BY CONCENTRATING ON THE SHORT TERM?

I appear to be Low in Time Frame. That means

_____

....

....

I appear to be High in Time Frame. That means

_____

....

....

I appear to be Mid-Range in Time Frame. That means

_____

....

....

Classification

Again, this is a reminder that a low score doesn't mean you cannot do or achieve something. Low Classification doesn't mean you can't work in fast-paced problem-solving environments, but it may mean that you find it stressful to have prolonged exposure in a fast-paced, ambiguous problem-filled position that does not give you time to draw upon your own experience.

LOW CLASSIFICATION	HIGH CLASSIFICATION
1. MAY FIND STRESSFUL WORK SITUATIONS THAT ARE CHRONICALLY CHAOTIC AND REQUIRE RAPID-FIRE PROBLEM-SOLVING	**1.** MAY BE EASILY BORED IN POSITIONS THAT REQUIRE MOSTLY ROTE OR ROUTINE WORK; THRIVES IN WORK ENVIRONMENTS THAT ARE MULTI-FACETED AND REQUIRE FAST-PACED PROBLEM-SOLVING
2. HAPPIER IN WORK SITUATIONS THAT HAVE SOME STRUCTURE AND PREDICTABILITY TO THE WORKDAY	**2.** LIKES CHANGE AND CHALLENGE, AND OPPORTUNITIES TO LEARN NEW THINGS IN AN ENVIRONMENT THAT HAS A LOT HAPPENING, PREFERABLY ALL AT ONCE
4. PATIENT WITH INDIVIDUAL DEVELOPMENT	**4.** IMPATIENT WITH INDIVIDUAL GROWTH AND DEVELOPMENT
5. APPROACHES NEW PROBLEMS FIRST AS OPPORTUNITIES TO APPLY PAST SOLUTIONS	**5.** LOVES TO SOLVE NEW PROBLEMS, LOTS OF THEM, AND TO THINK BEYOND THE DOTS"
6. ABLE TO LISTEN TO OTHERS WITHOUT ASSERTING OWN PROBLEM-SOLVING STYLE	**6.** REQUIRES A QUICK EXECUTIVE SUMMARY OF PROBLEM
7. CAN SEE THE CONTRIBUTIONS AND TALENTS OF OTHERS	**7.** MORE LIKELY TO FUNCTION IN ROLE OF CRITIC
8. PREFERS IMPLEMENTING PLANS	**8.** THRIVES ON FINDING THE FLAWS AND PROBLEMS IN PLANS, SYSTEMS OR PROCESSES

I appear to be Low in Classification. That means

_____

....

....

I appear to be High in Classification. That means

_____

....

....

I appear to be in the Mid-Range in Classification. That means

_____

....

....

LOW CONCEPT ORGANIZATION	HIGH CONCEPT ORGANIZATION
1. ABLE TO PLAN, ORGANIZE AND PRIORITIZE, BUT WITH EFFORT AND CONCENTRATION; ORGANIZING AND PLANNING ARE NOT NATURAL URGES	1. CAN SEE QUICKLY HOW ALL THE PIECES OF A PROJECT FIT TOGETHER IN LINEAR SEQUENCE
2. PREFERS TO HAVE THE EXTERNAL WORLD NEAT AND ORDERLY; A PLACE FOR EVERYTHING	2. ALL THOUGHTS AND MENTAL PROCESSES ARE WELL ORGANIZED, BUT DESK AND WORK AREA MAY NOT BE

LOW CONCEPT ORGANIZATION	HIGH CONCEPT ORGANIZATION
3. AN ADVANTAGE IN JOBS THAT REQUIRE INSTANT RESPONSE; ABLE TO SEE AROUND ANALYSIS AND GET TO THE BOTTOM LINE	**3.** INSISTS ON HAVING ALL RELEVANT INFORMATION BEFORE MAKING A DECISION; MAY MAKE DECISIONS SLOWLY AND PONDEROUSLY
4. MAY STRUGGLE WITH TASKS THAT REQUIRE METHODICAL THINKING	**4.** AN ADVANTAGE IN ANY KIND OF TASK THAT REQUIRES ANALYTICAL THINKING
5. NEEDS TO SPEND TIME EDITING AND ORGANIZING WRITTEN MATERIALS	**5.** FINDS IT EASY TO ORGANIZE INCOMING INFORMATION/ PROBLEMS LOGICALLY
6. NEEDS TOOLS LIKE TIME MANAGEMENT IN SELF-MANAGEMENT	**6.** ORGANIZING AND ALLOCATING PEOPLE AND RESOURCES IS RELATIVELY EASY
7. CAN BE QUICK AND DECISIVE	**7.** MAY PROCRASTINATE TO MAKE SURE EVERYTHING HAS BEEN THOUGHT THROUGH
8. DOESN T NEED TO SEE EVERY STEP OF A SOLUTION	**8.** NEEDS TO SEE AND UNDERSTAND ALL THE STEPS

I appear to be High in Concept Organization. That means

_____

....

....

I appear to be Low in Concept Organization. That means

_____

....

....

I appear to be Mid-Range in Concept Organization. That means

_____

....

....

LOW IDEA PRODUCTIVITY	HIGH IDEA PRODUCTIVITY
1. ABLE TO FOCUS ON ONE IDEA AT A TIME	**1.** MULTITUDE OF IDEAS MAKES IT HARDER TO FOCUS ON ONE
2. PREFERS A STABLE WORK ENVIRONMENT RATHER THAT A RAPIDLY CHANGING ONE	**2.** MAY BE RESTLESS AND DISSATISFIED IN ROLES THAT DEMAND ROUTINE TASKS AND ATTENTION TO DETAIL
3. LOOK FOR ROLES THAT EMPHASIZE ANALYSIS OF IDEAS, NOT THE FREQUENCY OF IDEAS	**3.** LOOK FOR ROLES THAT EMPHASIZE SPEED AND QUANTITY OF IDEAS; PICK AN ENVIRONMENT WITH PROBLEM-SOLVING AND PERSUASION AS MAJOR ROLES
4. PAYS ATTENTION TO DETAILS OF A TASK AND FOLLOWS THEM THROUGH TO CONCLUSION	**4.** TASKS THAT REQUIRE CONCENTRATION FOR LONG PERIODS OF TIME MAY BE CHALLENGING

LOW IDEA PRODUCTIVITY	HIGH IDEA PRODUCTIVITY
5. ABLE TO IMPLEMENT A GOAL OR VISION	**5.** CREATES ALTERNATIVE WAYS OF CONVEYING INFORMATION INSTEAD OF FOCUSING ON ONE
6. NEEDS TIME TO THINK OF IDEAS	**6.** THINKS OF IDEAS QUICKLY BUT NEEDS TO EDIT THEM BEFORE COMMUNICATING TO OTHERS
7. MAY FIND BRAINSTORMING WITH OTHERS TEDIOUS AND UNPRODUCTIVE	**7.** FINDS BRAINSTORMING ENERGIZING
8. ENJOYS STRUCTURE AND WELL-DEFINED ROLES	**8.** NEEDS TO SUPPLY INPUT AND COMMENTS ON WORK ASSIGNMENTS

I appear to be High in Idea Productivity. That means

_____

....

....

I appear to be Low in Idea Productivity. That means

_____

....

....

I appear to be Mid-Range in Idea Productivity. That means

_____

....

....

* * *

Integration of Personal Style and Problem-Solving (Decision-Making)

R eview your entries in my charts.

You now have data on your Personal Work Style (Generalist, Specialist, Introvert, Extrovert) as well as on your Time Frame, and some of your key Drivers (Classification, Concept Organization and Idea Productivity).

Using your insights, write a paragraph linking your Work Style and your Time Frame. For example: "I am a high Generalist. I thrive when I'm working on a team. I enjoy short term projects where I work with and through others.

"I look for environments that allow me to juggle many roles and processes at once. I find that speed of movement exhilarating! I am able to delegate parts of a project to others when the project calls for immediate results. Together, we succeed in solving problems that others have struggled with."

_____

_____

_____

_____

_____

_____

_____

_____

_____

_____

_____

_____

_____

_____

_____

_____

Now write a paragraph that describes how you use your problem-solving style. Here's an example:

"Because I am low in Classification and low in Concept Organization, I learn and solve problems by drawing upon my own experiences and knowledge.

"When a current problem is in an area I am familiar with, I can quickly diagnose and solve it. I am keenly aware of the strengths of others and I listen patiently to their suggestions and input. I am able to see roles in which they can be successful and help us.

"Early in my career, I tried many things and made many missteps. Over time, I developed a vast repository of experiences that enabled enabled me to assume positions of leadership. I can be incisive and decisive, especially when I can rely on past experience. My key strength is in identifying people's talents and placing them in roles where they can succeed."

_____

_____

_____

_____

_____

_____

_____

_____

_____

_____

_____

_____

_____

_____

Next, relate your high Idea Productivity to your work.

"With my high Idea Productivity, I find it easy to persuade people to my thinking, and I enjoy throwing ideas out to them. Selling a new idea or concept is key to my success at work. Of course, the rapid flow of ideas in my head can be distracting, especially when I have to concentrate on a particular job, but at least the pace of work is never dull.

"On the downside, I sometimes have trouble explaining a new idea to others. I need to slow down and wait until I have explained the idea so that it's clear to everyone. If I am managing a project, I need to let the others know when an idea is introduced as a trial balloon and is subject to debate and discussion.

"I try to work with people who are willing to throw out ideas simply to test them. I don't need to decide whose idea to go with until we have exhausted all the possibilities."

Now, write a statement that builds on your personal cluster of style and abilities.

Now that you have identified your Personal Style and three of your Drivers, and have combined them into your own statement, you need to look at your past roles and performance. First review your Time Line and look for connections and disconnections.

Upon reviewing your Career Development Time Line I suggest an additional exercise that I have found helpful at this point and that is completing an exercise I call Your Best Performance.

* * *

Exercise: Your Best Performance

Remember a time when you performed at your very best, and with great success. It's important to capture and recapture that moment in developing a Personal Vision based on your natural abilities.

Take 10 minutes to record what you remember as your PERSONAL BEST — as a leader, as a team contributor, or as an independent worker.

When did you perform at your very best? Was it with your present employer or with a previous employer? Was it in the private or public sector? Was it in high school or college? What was your role: Leader? Paid executive? Volunteer?

Try to these questions as examples in jogging your memory about your Best Performance:

I. Did you lead a team?
II. Did you resolve a crisis?
III. Did you "take over" after others had failed?
IV. Did you help victims in an accident or crisis?
V. Did you lead a task force in overhauling a system or a project?

VI. Did you plan or execute a merger of businesses or projects?

VII. Did you contribute or implement an important idea?

_____

_____

_____

_____

_____

_____

_____

_____

_____

_____

_____

_____

_____

_____

_____

_____

_____

_____

_____

_____

_____

_____

Now describe what you did and why you consider this experience your personal best. Remember, this is about you and your own abilities. Tell what you did personally.

_____

_____

_____

_____

_____

_____
_____
_____
_____

What words would you use to describe your feelings about this experience (pride, satisfaction, fulfillment, surprise)?

_____
_____
_____
_____
_____
_____
_____
_____
_____

List what steps you took, what your thoughts were, and what this tells us about your natural abilities.

_____
_____
_____
_____
_____
_____
_____
_____

Connect this experience to your increased knowledge of your abilities.

_____
_____
_____
_____

_____

_____

_____

_____

_____

_____

_____

What lessons did you come away with?

_____

_____

_____

_____

_____

_____

_____

_____

_____

Go back and look at your Integration Statement. Does your Best Performance confirm or challenge your perception of your abilities?

_____

_____

_____

_____

_____

_____

How can you use the knowledge you've acquired about yourself in your current and future work role(s)? What do you need to do more of? Less of?

_____

_____

_____

_____

_____

_____

_____

_____

_____

_____

_____

_____

_____

_____

_____

_____

_____

_____

_____

_____

_____

_____

_____

_____

HARDWIRED:

* * *

My Life with the Battery

I took the Battery when I was entering my 50s Turning Point. My private group practice, which depended heavily on insurance reimbursements, was being forced to rely more heavily on medication prescriptions, and I was becoming uncomfortable. I wanted a new direction for the next phase of my career! I needed to get off the stress cycle and figure out what I wanted to "do" in this next phase and "how" I would do it.

After two years of searching and six months of careful consideration and regular phone calls to the Atlanta office of The Highlands Company, I finally decided to take the leap and fly to Atlanta and take the Battery and get certified in its use.

Over the years, I had been through most, if not all, of the commonly used psychological assessments and had been trained by leaders in the acronym-rich field of Rorschach, TAT, WISC, Strong, MBTI and others not so well known. I approached the Battery with skepticism.

That skepticism – born and bred by my years in New York – grew as I knocked on the door at the Atlanta office at 7:45 for my 8 a.m. testing appointment. No answer! I had slept poorly in my hotel room the previous night, and my New York skepticism started to turn into something worse. Had I been scammed?

Five minutes later, the door was opened and I was greeted by a woman with a welcoming Georgia accent. She ushered me into the coffee room to wait until 8:15 for the 10 other participants who were coming to be trained!

The Battery was administered in a large room, with paper and pencil instead of on the Web, as it is now. The proctor sat in front of the room and gave us directions when to start, when to stop and when to turn the page. I thought, "Shades of the SAT, the Regents exams, and all the rest!!"

Four hours later, the Battery completed, I left for lunch, tired and depleted. I was sure the feedback session would prove that Emperor Tavantzis had no clothes, or at least that he was not qualified for anything except construction work.

My consultant was Margaret, known around the Highlands office as the Queen of Feedbacks. I may well have been assigned to her because I appeared so skeptical.

My first comment to her was that "you are probably going to tell me the only thing I would be good at is building houses." Queen Margaret responded: "Actually that is probably the last thing you should be considering." Now she had my attention!

My immediate reaction was to question all my results, but slowly the Queen brought me around and I started to "get" them.

First I had to overcome the idea that a low score in a work sample was always "bad." Then I had to get past the notion that everyone would score alike. (Why can't I perform as a Specialist and a Generalist anytime I want?) Margaret explained that my results showed that I was a Generalist/Extrovert, with low Classification, low Concept Organization, and high Idea Productivity.

As she explained what the results suggested about how I work, solve problems and make decisions, patterns from my past emerged to confirm her conclusions.

I recalled my first job at the Parkhurst Children's Shelter, an emergency placement center for abused children in Schenectady, N.Y., where, with my newly minted doctorate in counseling, I became the Executive Director. Suddenly, I was responsible for making decisions with little time to reflect, decisions that would affect children of all ages.

I suffered and agonized for months learning to make decisions without time to stop, think and gather data. My salvation was discovering that I had a talent for coming up with a variety of ideas for development of new programs, and then selling them to the community's leaders. I expanded the budget and could then hire people with talents that complemented mine, such as the ability to thrive in situations that demanded making decisions quickly without much information.

Another of the results that I challenged was my low score in Verbal Memory, which measures the ease with which you learn written material. I have always loved to read and I've sometimes had two or three books going at the same time. "OK," I thought, "what about that, Queen of Feedbacks?"

Margaret quietly made me realize that Verbal Memory was designed to measure the distinction between instant recall of written material and reading comprehension. She asked me if I could generally recall what I'd read. Her promptings made me realize a pattern that occurred when I taught my psychology courses. Even if I previously had read the text used when teaching, I was always amazed at what the re-reading of the material gave me. It was as though I was seeing the text for the first time! And that, my friends, is low Verbal Memory.

I finally accepted the Queen's conclusions and the Battery's findings. Over the next few years, I revisited my results often. I began to use the Battery in my practice and apply its lessons (go back and see the summary paragraphs I wrote in earlier parts of Test Drives that describe me). I used my new insights to assist others. I tried to communicate how others could use what I had learned. It became clear to me over time that the Ability Battery had confirmed what I should have known about myself, what I had been doing in my daily decision-making .and what roles had brought me satisfaction in my work.

It was there all along —in sight but not clearly seen.

I have also learned to take on roles and new situations that allow me to contribute what I am good at. Over the years, I have seen over and over that I have the ability to select talented people and then place them in roles where they can contribute best. I am also pulled to work roles that permit me to generate lots of ideas and come up with instant alternatives and solutions. Additionally, I am action-oriented and decisive in situations in which I have experience.

In my early years with Highlands, I was very flattered by being described as the *Odysseus* of the Highlands program. Odysseus was, of course, legendary for arriving at novel solutions to overwhelming problems. Managing oneself, as Peter Drucker has said, is the key to success. I have tried to stay away from roles that require high focus and follow-through. When these roles confront me, I make sure to surround myself with people who can complement me. When I have to stay focused for long periods of time, I know to intersperse them with periods of interaction and idea generation with others.

It is challenging to work in a world in which you can apply your knowledge to empower and catalyze others. However, we will see that staid tradition and old-style top-down managers still hold sway, holding on to centralized decision-making. Or when lip service is paid to the principle "Have people work from their strengths," but no clear methodology exists to make it a reality.

More often than not, what I hear from clients is that their managers often see only one dimension of their abilities and assign them again and again to the same job. No one can be expected to know all the complexities in another person's abilities and personality. It is really up to each of us to articulate how our talents can best be used, and then, if we find ourselves continually "knocking on the deaf man's door," we may need to find another way or a new role.

Another ongoing challenge has been my low Grip score. Surprisingly, my score was not a shock when I was assessed in Atlanta so many years ago. I have always had a tendency to throw my hands up when I find something to be more difficult than I initially thought.

Over time I have learned to compensate, to leave a frustrating problem for a time and then come back to it. I have also accepted the fact that I need down time to recuperate after exerting prolonged effort. I have adjusted fairly well here. In fact, at a recent book-signing party held for me, one of the invitees – a much-admired senior executive – commented about my tenacity in sticking to the development of my business!

Over the years, my Battery results have seemed less and less surprising and more an accurate reflection of who and what I am. I have grown into knowing my strengths and recognizing my challenges. I hope that others taking this same path of discovery will do so as well.

EPILOGUE
PARTING WORDS

In this small book, I have tried to show the power in discovering and knowing one's strengths. In the very articulation of who you are, you will understand the story of your life and focus on your talents. You will envision and plan for a future in which you can be both satisfied and happy.

I wish you good luck on this path of discovery and hope I have provided you with some new insights to help you along the way. If you need support on your journey, you may want to check in periodically at "http://www.imdleadership.com" for inspirational tales and video clips of others on similar journeys!

ACKNOWLEDGMENTS

This book was awhile in the making. It took several years and many false and painful starts and rejections to get it published.

I would like to thank everyone who supported me in this project, and especially everyone who read and commented on the drafts of this book: my wife, Martha; my daughter, Eleni; my sister-in-law, Mary Kehoe; my former students Marybeth Thornbury, Clare Sautter and Quesia Brower. My special thanks to Mary Ruggiero for her in-depth editorial comments. And a special thanks to the late Lazar Emanuel who put in many hours editing the earlier version of this book as well as the time he provided in making sure all my Highlands related writing is clear. I want also to acknowledge the help of all my clients and graduate students over the years who sharpened the ideas presented in this book, as well as my teachers and mentors of many years ago, Drs. Vasso Vassiliou and George Vassiliou, and Walt Lifton.

In this book I introduce the Eight Factors that are the basis of a career and life vision. It is impossible not to be influenced by each of these factors and how they intertwine into your career and life work! This book reflects clearly where I am in my Career Development stage, as well as my Abilities, Values, Skills, Interests, Personal Style, Goals and Family of Origin.

I want to thank Kim Mumola and Susan Shipwash of The Highlands Company for their assistance and support in publishing this work.

I also want to thank my clients over the years who have contributed to my development and understanding of how the Highlands Ability Battery works. Following a long clinical tradition, the case studies in this book are based on actual sessions with people whose identifying details have been altered to protect their identities.

My special thanks to Paul Jablow, my colleague and my ghost writer, who was able to take what I wanted to say and skillfully convey it in my voice but in a way that the reader could follow! Paul's patience, sense of humor, writing skill and intelligence make this a book that you will find helpful.

Of course, I can't do an acknowledgment without mentioning my Family of Origin. The decision by my parents to move our family to Greece when I was young had a profound impact on the person I have become. I thank each of them for the cultural richness and atmosphere this provided.

On a more personal level, I want to express my special thanks to my loving wife, Martha, who has found the time in her busy career to be supportive and to give critical takes on my work.

I have tried to convey for the reader the excitement and significance of knowing our natural abilities and using our knowledge over the course of our lives and careers. If I have failed to get you excited about your natural abilities and starting on the journey of developing a vision for yourself, the fault is ultimately mine and no one else's.

Taking The Battery

To take the Battery, please contact me directly at http://www.imdleadership.com/.

I will provide a 20 percent discount to off the retail price of the Battery and your first feedback conference. if you have taken the Battery and want someone else to experience it, please ask him or her to contact me at please contact me directly at http://www.imdleadership.com/."

Executive Coaching

Working with companies, we align your goals with the strengths of your employees to achieve maximum results.

Successful iMD Leadership clients include Comcast Spotlight, Glaxo SmithKline, PJM interconnection, and Novartis

For further information, please contact me directly at: http://www.imdleadership.com/.

Individual Coaching

Interested individual can contract for individual coaching conducted virtually by Dr. Tavantzis.

Personal Strategic Planning Seminars

These small group (5-7 participants) 10 week interactive webinars will take participants through our process that starts with the Ability Battery and ends with an integrative Career vision for each individual.

Please visit our website for more information or contact me directly Thomas.tavantzis@imdleadership.com

Made in the USA
Middletown, DE
09 January 2017